The illustrated
Spirit
of the
Home

'Sue,
            our very dear friend
wishing you lots of love & success,
and a very happy home (you will find it!)

                    all our love
                    Frances
                        &
                    Duncan

The illustrated
Spirit
of the
Home

How to make your home
a sanctuary

Jane Alexander
Photographs by Tim Goffe

Thorsons
An Imprint of HarperCollinsPublishers

Thorsons
An Imprint of HarperCollins*Publishers*
77–85 Fulham Palace Road
Hammersmith, London W6 8JB

The Thorsons website address is:
www.thorsons.com

Published by Thorsons 1999

10 9 8 7 6 5 4 3 2 1

Editorial work: Donna Wood

© Jane Alexander 1999
Photographs © Tim Goffe

Jane Alexander asserts the moral right to
be identified as the author of this work

A catalogue record for this book is available
from the British Library

ISBN 0 7225 3717 4

Printed and bound in Hong Kong

contents

permissions

Grateful acknowledgment is made for permission to quote material from the following works:

Facing the World with Soul by Robert Sardello, copyright Robert Sardello 1992, used by permission of Lindisfarne Books, Hudson, NY12534

Memories, Dreams, Reflections by C. G. Jung, Random House Inc. (US, Canada and open market), HarperCollins Publishers (UK)

Pagan Meditations by Ginette Paris, Spring Publications

The Fragrant Pharmacy by Valerie Ann Worwood, Macmillan General Books

The Physics of Angels by Matthew Foz and Rupert Sheldrake, HarperCollins Publishers Inc.

Owning Your Own Shadow by Robert Johnson. Copyright © 1991 by Robert A. Johnson. HarperCollins Publishers Inc.

The Pregnant Virgin by Marion Goodman, Inner City Books

The Bloomsbury Encyclopaedia of Aromatherapy by Chrissie Wildwood published by Bloomsbury Publishing Plc in 1996

Sacred Space by Denise Linn, Rider

The House as Mirror of Self by Clare Cooper Marcus, copyright © 1995 by Clare Cooper Marcus, reprinted by permission from Conari Press

The Natural House Book by David Pearson by permission of Gaia Books Ltd, London

Creating Sacred Space with Feng Shui by Karen Kingston reproduced and adapted by kind permission of the author and Piatkus Books

Care of the Soul by Thomas Moore, Piatkus Books (UK and Commonwealth), HarperCollins Publishers

Places of the Soul by Christopher Day, HarperCollins Publishers

acknowledgements

Jane Alexander

This is not a book which was 'built' single-handedly so I would like to give heartfelt thanks to the following builders, plumbers and interior decorators of the soul: Sarah Dening for her perennial support and friendship and, in particular, for her invaluable insights into Jung's typology and the house. Sarah Shurety and Liz Williams, my feng shui geniuses - thanks for keeping my chi flowing smoothly. Denise Linn and Karen Kingston, the two great space clearers, who have been so generous with their time, wisdom and inspiration over the years. Jim Bultman, a wonderful e-mail correspondent, for his help in tracing Hestia. Adrian and James, Monty and Bear - all my love, dear souls. Chris and Alice for their support over the years - looking forward to having you this side of the Atlantic! Judy Chilcote - many "gratitude moments" for being way more than an agent - a Friend (with a capital F) who does all the tough stuff. Tim Goffe for his stunning photographs which capture far more eloquently than all my words the true spirit of the home. Belinda Budge for being the editor of my dreams, full of sensible advice, soaring inspiration, spirit, soul and friendship. Michele Turney for her excellent early editing. Adrian Morris for his excellent design work. Nicky Vimpany for acts of extreme coordination. Donna Wood for grappling womanfully with my wilful text. Megan Slyfield and Hattie Madden for their support and encouragement. And everyone else at Thorsons, especially the unsung heroes of the sales team who make sure this book ends up where it was always meant to be: in your hands and hopefully in your home.

Tim Goffe

Firstly I would like to thank Jane for her book and her part in the transformation of my home. I would like to thank Belinda and Nicky to name but two of the outstandingly helpful staff at Thorsons. I would like to thank all my clients, friends and homeowners that have let me into their houses and made me cups of tea. Special thanks is also due to Toni and Jill, Rick and Heidi, Karen Howes, Patrick, Peter Cocks, and all my suffering assistants (more tea acknowledgement here).

I would also like to thank the following for permission to photograph the designs included in this book:

S.F. at Hudson Featherstone Architects pages 2 and 116; Paxton Locher Architects pages 9, 37, 45, 62, 80, 83, 101, 102, 128, 131, 135 and 169; Tim Bushe Associates pages 13, 62, 76, 99, 132 and 134; Baker Nevile Designs pages 16, 17, 30, 33, 47, 59, 69, 71, 106, 123, 127, 137, 161, 177 and 178; Francoise de Pfyffer Designs; pages 57, 120, 149, 173 and 174; The Douglas Stevens Partnership pages 59 and 66; Mark Wilmot, William Lasdun pages 68 and 164; Meath Baker Design page 79; McDowell + Benedetti pages 82 and 86; Robert Dye Associates page 105; Habitat - Dinn Associates page 114; private collection, Peter Cocks pages 143, 144, 145, 152 and 163; paintings by Kitty North pages 33 and 48.

And lastly I would like to thank Sue my wife for sharing in the ups and downs of a freelance career and being so supportive, to this end I dedicate my part in this book to her.

All photographs © Tim Goffe

The publishers would like to thank the Lucky Feng Shui Company, Ballard House, 37 Norway Street, Greenwich, London SE10 9DD, for providing bamboo flutes and the ba-gua mirror pictured on page 91.

introduction

almost all of us have somewhere we call home. Whether it's a large, grand house or simply a corner in a shared room, if we're lucky we have a place we can claim as our own. Each and every one of us sees home in a different way: some of us might claim we barely think about home – it's simply a place out of the elements where we eat and sleep. Others would insist that home is a vital part of life: a solid center in which we can feel safe and secure. Yet more of us regard our homes as a symbol of taste and status, a means of indulging creativity or proving our social standing. However we experience home there is no doubt that the places in which we live are becoming more and more important to us. There is a huge proliferation of interest in houses, home-building, interior design and decoration. The news-stands are full to bursting with magazines on homes and gardens; coffee tables groan with glossy books showing perfect homes. Turn on the television and someone will be telling you how to revamp a kitchen or hide a radiator.

There's far more to this than simply another fashionable trend. We have a deep collective yearning for an idealized image of home – for ideal homes. It's as though we feel that if we could only make our homes look right, they would somehow *be* right. We would live perfect lives in our perfect homes. But if we think we can create a happy home from the pages of a magazine, if we think we can buy our way to a healing home, we are deluding ourselves.

A PROFOUND LONGING

This almost desperate interest in the external trappings of home – the newest colors, the latest furniture, the best cooker, the freshest curtains – disguises a more profound longing. In our hearts we want to come home to a real home. A real home is a place that nurtures us on every level. It gives us the creature comforts that make our bodies feel relaxed and comfortable. It provides the safety and serenity that allow our minds and emotions peace and security. Above all, it nourishes our souls. A real home is not a show-home packed to the gills with expensive furniture, decorated by the most fashionable interior designer: it is a living space that has the power to make us feel safe in a troubled world. It is our refuge, our sanctuary – a place we can walk into and feel a sense of relief and relaxation as we shut the world behind us.

Some homes do this automatically. Others need our help. Sadly, over recent years we have been neglecting our homes or, more accurately, we've been ignoring the spirits of our homes. A home is far more than a physical structure; it is a living entity with a soul of its own. In the past the home was honored as a deity – it was considered to have its own spirit and a host of attending spirits. All over the globe people acknowledged and venerated their homes, treating them with love and respect. Not to do so would be to bring trouble and strife on the house and its inhabitants. Nowadays we treat our homes poorly. Often we allow them to become dirty, cluttered and neglected. And even when we do carefully maintain and preserve the home, we run into the danger of turning our homes into stiff, stilted places of fashion and decorum – they look good but they don't necessarily feel good. These 'look-good' houses exist because we have left out one vital part of the equation: we have ignored the home's vital living energy, its spirit.

We cannot achieve true peace of mind and spirit unless we reconnect with our homes at this deeper level. Without a true home we have no barrier between us and the ever-increasing stress of everyday life and work. A home with a heart embraces us when we walk through the door; we can almost feel it wrap its healing around us.

Its aim and purpose is to protect and soothe, to bring us home in every sense. So one of the most important tasks we can perform for our physical and psychological health is to, quite literally, come home.

THE ART OF HOME MAKING

But we seem to have lost the old instinctive art of home-making in its truest, most ancient form. We know how to arrange pictures but not how to make a house feel warm and welcoming. We are experts in knocking out fireplaces but amateurs when it comes to putting in atmosphere and feeling. Looking at the often sterile spaces we call home can be depressing and can bring on feelings of hopelessness. But we can easily change the situation. Our home-making skills haven't really been lost – they are simply crafts which have become rusty through disuse. We can swiftly relearn the steps to creating a true home, to ensouling the home. All it takes is a little time and effort – and a large dose of imagination and wonder. What is needed is nothing less

The glow of polished wood, a crisp cloth and splashes of vibrant color create a lived-in atmosphere in this kitchen.

than the re-enchantment of our homes – to endow them with magic, warmth and joy. We need to bring back the life and soul of the home, honor its power and healing, respect its spirit.

It's a case of relearning the old ways: how to cleanse not just the physical fabric of the house, but its spiritual energy too; how to sense and alter atmosphere; how to intuit what your home needs and what it doesn't want at all. Rediscovering the spirit of your home is about bringing the natural world into your space, giving play to all the elements and the life force they embody. It's about allowing your senses full rein: filling your home with delicious sounds and scents, textures and tastes.

On an even deeper level, the spirit of your home can help you find out about yourself – who you are and who you'd like to be. Your home represents who you are, and by changing your surroundings you can certainly start the process of becoming someone closer to your true, authentic Self. It's a journey of discovery and transformation that can alter your entire life. Finally, you arrive back where you always wanted to be. You come home.

PUTTING THE HEART BACK INTO YOUR HOME

The aim of this book is to show you how to turn a simple home into a true sanctuary – a place of laughter, joy, peace and welcome. Many of the ideas in this book are almost too obvious to be true. They are simple, straightforward commonsense. You'll have that feeling of 'well, of course, I knew that' – and you did, you do. We all know this information at some level in our psyche because it is our common heritage.

Whether you believe in past lives, the collective unconscious or the simple laws of genetics, we have all venerated the home in our pasts: we have all nurtured the sacred flame of the hearth, the symbolic Mother, the earth. At some level in our psyche we know all about honoring the spirits of the home, of 'cleansing' space as well as cleaning floors, of filling a sacred space with healing color, sound and light.

But at a more conscious level we are maybe not so sure. While much of this book is common sense, other ideas might sound far-fetched and even ludicrous to those with an overly rational mind. If you find such esoteric ideas difficult, don't worry. You can still have a healing, soulful home without understanding or even believing a word of the theory or the mystical side of the equation.

Use this book as a resource, an ideas manual – dip in and out of it as you like. If you become bogged down in theory, psychology and mythology simply skip Part One. Spend some time with Part Two if you can, because thinking about home in the ways suggested there can really change the way you look on yourself and your expectations of home. But, again, it's not totally necessary. If you're a really down-to-earth kind of person who just wants to get on with it, head straight for Part Three which is where the pure practical work begins. Take it slowly – you can't change everything at once – and remember that every house has its individual personality. Some are old and grumpy like crotchety grandparents and need handling carefully and diplomatically. Others have a younger, brasher attitude and can take more of a fresh sweep of the broom. But whatever your home, do take this opportunity to put the heart back into it. As Dorothy says in *The Wizard of Oz*, 'There's no place like home.'

Below An eclectic collection of well-loved items amassed over the years adds to the home's feeling of soulfulness.

the spirit of the home

the security of home

Why do we need a home so badly? How come, when we talk about our worst nightmares, many of us will shudder and say that the most terrible thing we could imagine would be to lose our homes, to become homeless, to live on the streets? Why is it that homeless people are often considered the worst pariahs of society? Few people feel comfortable looking on the homeless – we may call it guilt or pity but most of us scuttle past, or try to ignore homelessness. Why such an extreme reaction? Is it that homelessness, not having a home, a base, is such a deep, in-built fear that many of us project our terror out onto those who are homeless?

Statistics show that homes are very much on our minds nowadays, with increasing emphasis being put on them. More of us in the West own our homes than ever before. We spend more money on fixing our homes, and one of the most popular hobbies is home improvement. Whereas in the past we might have boasted of going on exotic holidays or buying flashy cars, now we impress our friends with our new sofa, with a fresh coat of paint, with a new alarm system. It seems that now, maybe more than ever before, we need to feel the security of our homes. It's not hard to see why. Our working lives are becoming ever less secure – few people nowadays can count on a job for life. With divorce rates soaring there is little certainty in our relationships. And as our knowledge of space and the cosmos deepens, we can no longer rely on being at the center of a gentle, embracing universe. Life is becoming psychologically very frightening. Someone once asked Einstein, 'What is the most important question you can ask in life?' He replied, 'Is the universe a friendly place or not?' In the past we trusted that the universe was friendly: at the very least we saw ourselves as an important and large part of the universe. But now we are less certain. Space is almost utterly unknown. We may be alone in infinity, which is frightening enough. Even more scary is the thought that we might not be alone and that our fellow inhabitants might not be gentle, evolved ET-like beings.

It's a strange feeling for us – this uncertainty. In the last few centuries we have been growing in confidence almost by the minute. Technology has given us greater control over our environment; we have thought ourselves masters of the Earth and everything in it. We merrily plundered the planet's resources without a regard for the future and then, once we started heading up out of the Earth to the moon and beyond, our arrogance knew no limits. So what if we destroyed the Earth? Undoubtedly there would be another planet 'out there' we could colonize. Our planet, our home, became disposable. We turned our backs on Earth and turned our sights towards new places. We headed for the sun. The very name of the space missions, Apollo, drums home the fact. Apollo, or Helios, is the god of the sun – bright, shining, new, outgoing and outreaching, a very masculine energy which always thrusts upwards, away from Earth, the warm, embracing, feminine energy of the goddess.

THE HEARTH – CENTER OF THE HOME

In order to understand what this has to do with our physical homes, we need to look back in time, to how the ancients perceived home and the Earth. The very first concept of home was the hearth, the fire that cooked and warmed and kept us safe from wild beasts and cast light into the dread of darkness. This original fire was always round in shape – as if our ancestors knew that the Earth itself was also spherical. In Ancient Greece the structure

Powerful animals such as large dogs, dragons and lions depicted in stone make excellent guardians – what stranger would dare approach this converted farm building?

known as an omphalos was originally a fire banked and covered with earth – a glowing heart, surrounded by the earth. It was considered to be the navel of Gaia, the Earth Mother. Later it came to be represented as a rounded mound of stones, but its symbolism was the same: it demonstrated the link between us and the Earth. Examples can be found, not just in Greece, but all over the world.

So the round hearth became a powerful symbol of home, the center of every sacred space and, by extension, a symbol of the sacred Earth itself. Since time immemorial the circle has been seen as a symbol of wholeness, of the complete psyche, the fullness of the Self. The Eastern mandala represents the path to the center, to individuation, to becoming 'whole' in soul. Mazes, spirals, labyrinths, circles of standing stones – they all lead from the outside to the inner mystery. The circle is the hidden heart: it is where the mystics find their gods or goddesses and where others simply find their soul.

The first houses were also round, continuing this close link and honoring our essential connection with Mother Earth. When the great psychologist Carl Jung built his house at Bollingen he based the design on a simple African hut.

> *At first I did not plan a proper house but merely a kind of primitive one-storey dwelling. It was to be a round structure with a hearth in the center and bunks along the walls. I more or less had in mind an African hut where the fire, ringed with stone, burns in the middle and the whole life of the family revolves around this center. Primitive huts concretize an idea of wholeness, a familial wholeness…*
>
> Carl Jung, Psychologist

Jung expanded his basic hut into a two-storey tower – but kept the round shape and the central hearth. He commented that, 'the feeling of repose and renewal that I had in this tower was intense from the start. It represented for me the maternal hearth.'

architecture for the soul

just because we are modern people, living fast, furious lives, it does not stop these archetypes resonating within us. In recent years some far-sighted psychologists and philosophers have recognized that we need to rediscover and respect the archetypes within our homes. 'Every home is a microcosm, the archetypal "world" embodied in a house or plot of land or an apartment,' says Thomas Moore. 'A real home is always at once a particular place and the entire world.' Note he says a 'real' home – in other words a home made potent and numinous by the love and

feeling we invest in it. 'Show'-homes just won't do it. We all know those kind of places – buildings which are built and designed so full of pride and prestige that you feel uncomfortable the moment you walk in. You barely like to sit down in case you crease the cushions. These are the kind of homes that make you stand to attention; that make children and animals unwelcome and adults feel ill at ease. They symbolize a complete breakdown between the owner and the Earth – the link is simply not recognized. But anyone with sensitivity of soul can feel it in their bones. The place is not a home, it is a statement – like the latest designer clothes or the smartest sports car. It is hollow.

THE SYMBOLISM OF THE HOME

A home, then, is a symbol of the world, our own mini-world, our own Mother Earth. When we feel safe and comfortable in our homes then we feel more able to deal with the often frightening outside world. When we start to remember this link consciously and honor our homes in the manner they

When architecture becomes 'egotecture' we live and work in inflated, hollow, monotonous, self-reliant, flashy, defiant space.

The image of the home invokes archetypal, permanent aspects of Earth connected with the desire to feel at home in the world. The home is more than a box in which to live; it is a soul activity to be retrieved from the numbness of the world of modern objects. Each place of the house, each room, hallway, closet, stair and alcove is a distinct structure that animates different aspects of soul.

Robert Sardello, Psychotherapist

deserve, which befits such a powerful protective force, we will change our relationship, not only with our homes but also with our wider home, the planet herself. We don't have to deny our desire for the sky, the heavens and the sun – nobody would want to stay always Earthbound. But a home can be the meeting point between Earth and sky. In classical symbolism the circle was the symbol of the Earth. The square, a four-sided structure, is considered to be the symbol of order, stability and control. So it's not surprising that we started to build our homes in square and rectangular structures: we were trying to impose order, trying to control the Earth, to make ourselves feel safe. Unfortunately, these shapes with their pointed corners are not as energetically harmonious as the earlier round houses (as is shown in the later sections on space clearing and feng shui). But as few of us are likely to be living in rounded houses, we just have to learn how to deal with our corners.

Now notice the next symbolic shape of the house – the slanting roof. All over the world you will see roofs which slant downward. In

practical terms they allow the rain to fall swiftly away from the roof. In symbolic terms, however, the slanting roof is akin to the pyramid shape pointing toward heaven. So the house sits between the Earth and heaven: it offers us a link between the Mother Earth and the Father Sky; between Gaia and God. Again, this was something our ancestors knew all too well. Thomas Moore notes that throughout the world you will find houses decorated with suns and moons, stars and even a dome to reflect the sweep of the cosmos. By adorning the house in such a way, our ancestors would always remember their links: to the Earth via the hearth and to the cosmos via the representations of the stars.

All this shows us why, at its most profound level, a house is always going to be more than just a structure. Deep in our psyches we recognize that a house stands for far more than mere shelter. Understanding that our home is, symbolically, the world turns even the humblest space into a place full of mythic resonance, of deep archetypal power. No wonder the ancients venerated their homes: a touch of this awe and wonder is the first step to putting the spirit back into your home.

The slick, clean lines of a state-of-the-art kitchen can be softened by the addition of certain items; here, chairs with curving lines, a retro clock and fresh flowers do the trick.

hestia, abandoned goddess

I f home is such an essential symbol for our souls, why have we so neglected it in recent years? First and foremost, we simply haven't had time. We've been so busy living 'out there' in the world that we haven't had a chance to turn our eyes, ears, feelings, inward. The world is getting smaller, and more accessible, by the moment. An exciting holiday used to mean piling along to the nearest seaside town or camping in some wilderness within a day's drive or so. Now we can travel the world, see places our grandparents could only read about in books. We jump on

a plane and land in a different time zone, a different country, a completely different culture – the world is truly our oyster. We needn't even leave our homes to travel the world. We can log onto the Internet, connecting within seconds with people in the opposite hemisphere to our own, jumping from continent to continent as the fancy takes us.

Apollo is not the only ruling archetype of our time. We are living in the age of Hermes, or Mercury, the winged messenger of the gods, the expert communicator, who thrives on speed and intellect. Hermes, you could say, is the god of the telephone (or even better, the mobile phone), the fax, the computer (and especially the lap-top). He is the god of the media, of television and radio, newspapers and magazines; the Lord of the Internet. His currency is information, the more of it the better. His mode of transmission is quick, very quick. We have fallen in love with Hermes, with his quick, agile mind, his restless, seeking nature, his charming yet deceptive trickster qualities. Hermes is the god of the fast buck, the conscience of the workaholic, the goad of the person who says more, just a little more. We all need Hermes in our lives

(without him existence can become very dull) but we are running the risk of toppling too far into his frenetic realm.

We are suffering from information overload. It is not mentally possible for us to take in all the information, the news and views that are thrown at us without a break, day in, day out. When was the last time you spent a whole weekend with no phones, no papers, no television or radio – shut away from the frenetic outside world?

No-one is suggesting that you have to live like a hermit, or give up your phone or your computer. But we need to have a balance; something to counteract this one-sided worship of Hermes.

Fortunately there is a natural antidote to Hermes' frenetic information highway. Her name is Hestia. Hestia (to the Greeks) or Vesta (to the Romans) is the classical goddess of the hearth and home. In Hestia we find the balance needed to offset Hermes' madness. He races around; she stays put. He looks for the new; she revels in the order of the known. He lures us out into the world, stretching ourselves further and further; she urges us back to the center, focusing on the deep, quiet needs of the soul.

Left **Nothing represents the heart of the home better than the flames of a roaring log fire – it is the symbol of the goddess Hestia, once worshipped in every household, now sadly abandoned.**

Above **In Greek and Roman times statues of the goddesses were far more commonplace than they are today. They served to remind people of the ties that exist between us, the Earth, our homes and the gods.**

HESTIA, FOCUS OF THE HOME

Although Hestia was very rarely represented in figurative form, she was understood to be present in the heart of every home, in the glowing embers of the household hearth. She was the fire at the center of the home, the spirit of the home, its organizing soul.

Hestia has a long lineage – she is not just a classical goddess. As far back as archaeologists have discovered remains of human life, they have found evidence of a cult of the hearth and the home fire. Stephanie A. Demetrakopoulos, writing in *Spring* (1979), notes that the nomadic Vedic Indians were celebrating a cult of the 'world' fire back in 1000–2000 *BC*. The fire bound the worshipper to the Earth and to his family; the rituals represented the ties that exist between people, the Earth, their home and the gods. So Hestia has a long and honorable heritage.

By the time the Greek and Roman civilizations came into being, the worship of the goddess of the hearth and home was of the utmost importance. Hestia was not a showy goddess: she had none of the glamor of Aphrodite or Helios, the power and majesty of Zeus and Hera, the mystery of Persephone or the frenetic energy of

Hermes. Like Athena and Artemis, Hestia was a virgin goddess but, while her sister goddesses were active in the worlds of both humans and gods, Hestia did not bother herself with politics or the ways of the world. She had her place and was content to be there – not surprising, really, seeing as she was worshipped as the center of every home, and every town. For while every individual home had its hearth sacred to Hestia so every town had its own Hestia, a central sanctuary where the fire, the living heart, burned to give the town or city its center, its connection to the Earth. Such places were totally sacred: anyone who sought sanctuary within the temple walls was kept safe. So you can appreciate how, even at this early time, the ideas of home and sanctuary, a place where you were literally safe from the world, came together quite naturally.

Hestia was central to everyday Greek and Roman life. She gave the house its soul. Stephanie Demetrakopoulos quotes a Homeric hymn to Hestia which seems to show how keen houseowners were to have her blessing:

Hestia…come on into this house of mine, come on in here with shrewd Zeus,
Be gracious towards my song.

'A house or temple…seems only to be a building until it receives its Hestian soul,' comments Demetrakopoulos. In ancient Greece the Hestian soul was put into the house in the most literal way. When a young woman married and set up her own home her mother would light a torch at her own household hearth and carry it before the bride and bridegroom to their new house, lighting their new fire with it. Then Hestia was deemed to have come to dwell in the daughter's house. A similar custom can be found in Russia, where the household spirit of the hearth was known as a *domovik*. If the family moved house, they would carry brands from the old stove and light the stove in the new house from them. An invocation is spoken over the stove to provide a welcome for the *domovik*.

Left **Here, the hearth is the true focus of the room; the position of the furniture and the classical carvings of the fireplace give it extra weight and importance.**

This custom has also been retained by modern Western pagans. When moving to a new house, they practice the ritual of taking with them a glowing log from their old fire and putting it in the fireplace of the new house. This serves as a link between the old house and the new.

So Hestia imbues a house with spirit; her hearth provides the essential link with the Earth. She also provides safety, security and serenity. She brings together the people who live in a house – whether one or many – in an atmosphere of warmth and shelter.

She is a sociable goddess: she presided over the preparation of meals and the first mouthful of the meal was always consecrated to her. In Roman times 'To Vesta' was a common grace. But, although she can be seen, in one way, as the representative of Mother Earth, she is not a 'mothering' goddess. Hestia always remained a virgin, her own woman, self-reliant and inward-looking. Her mood is one of quiet introspection and absorption which is why she is such an obviously healthy balance when we have too much Hermetic energy whizzing around in our lives.

Above **If you do not have an old-fashioned hearth then look for the spirit of Hestia at your kitchen stove; the modern-day heart of the home, where families tend to congregate.**

THE NEGLECTED HEARTH

But Hestia has been abandoned; we have forgotten her place at the center of the house. Often her hearth has been blocked in and her heat dissipated through a central heating system. The center of our homes is more frequently the computer than the fireside; the television than the dining table. Those who live on their own often stick a meal in a microwave and eat it on their laps in front of the television. Those with families throw food at children as they disappear through the door to their own activities, hardly exchanging a word as they pass by.

How many of us can say, hand on heart, that we actually sit and center ourselves at a table to eat? How many of us sit in front of a living fire to dream? Who, nowadays, sits in a circle and sings, or tells stories, or plays music around a camp fire? And who would confess to doing housework in an almost meditative state of self-absorption? All these are Hestia's joys. But it is easy to see how Hestia has been lost.

She is simply not flashy enough, not sexy enough, not exciting enough. To early feminists, Hestia was anathema. She represented everything that women should be rebelling against. Hestia was a timid little housewife; an introverted, repressed little stay-at-home rabbit hiding in her warren. Women quite rightly wanted, after centuries of repression, to get out there into the world, to model themselves on more exciting archetypes: sexually confident and demanding Aphrodite; wise, intelligent, cool Athena; proud, independent, feisty Artemis. We turned our backs on Hestia and she became a forgotten goddess. Women went out into the world and proved that they are as good as men, as capable and, if need be, as ruthless and ambitious. But when we turned our backs on Hestia we lost something monumental. We lost our sense of focus, our powers of discrimination. We also lost our haven. Nowadays women are beginning to notice that something is missing. They have demanding jobs;

Turning our backs on Hestia's old-fashioned values can lead us to feel cold and empty inside. Our busy, modern lives can lack focus unless we can learn to redress the balance, welcome Hestia back into our lives and relight her fires.

they artfully juggle family and career; but often they have lost the true spirit of their homes.

We are too busy, caught in the Hermes trap, to give ourselves the time we need to center, to focus on what is truly important to us. Interesting, that word focus – it's a Latin word which means the hearth, Hestia's domain.

Nobody would suggest that women should give up their jobs and get back into the kitchen, but it is true that many women need to put themselves back in touch with their Hestian values. They need to give themselves the time and space they need for quiet

> *'If we had a feminism that caused us to get out of the house, is there not also room for feminism that would bring us back home, so that our homes would reflect ourselves and would once more have a soul?'*
>
> Ginette Paris, Social Psychologist

reflection, for musing, for pottering. They need to have a home which renews them so they can rejoin the battle out there in the modern world refreshed and with a sense of vigor and serenity, as Ginette Paris reinforces in her words about feminism.

Although it may sound like it, this isn't an issue just for women. In the old form of patriarchal society, a man could automatically expect to find Hestia in the home. The woman who invested all her life into her home was a natural devotee of the goddess, and the 'contented husband' could expect to come home to a warm, welcoming home with fire blazing, everything spick-and-span and a nice hot dinner on the table. All this providing the woman was a 'contented wife' of course – and many weren't (too much Hestia is not a good thing either!) But now our society is very different, and while modern women have to rediscover Hestia, modern men have an even greater challenge – of starting their own relationship with the goddess of the home.

HERMES & HESTIA IN HARMONY

Everyone, woman or man, needs the protection of Hestia. Hestia was, and can be, the guardian of the house – it is she who makes the space sacred, who demands that sometimes we close the doors and windows to the world and devote our time to focusing inwards on ourselves, our family, our home. She is the one who says 'enough', who could turn off the television and start a conversation; who could pick up a book instead of logging onto the Web; who might insist on shared family meal-times rather than TV dinners. She is the one who can put tricky Hermes in his place. Interestingly, the Greeks understood perfectly the dynamic between Hermes and Hestia.

While Hestia governed the house itself, Hermes guarded the door, the threshold. He was often represented by a phallic-shaped stone, known as a 'herm'. He looked outwards into the world; she focused inwards. In some two-headed statues of door guardians there are representations, not of Janus, but of Hermes and Hestia.

Left **A house governed by Hestia will still need some Hermian influences. This unusual horned door guardian will protect the house and perfectly represents the masculine energy of Hermes. A more usual representation of the god is a phallic-shaped stone, sometimes called a 'herm'.**

One looks out, the other looks in. They are in perfect balance. This is the model we need for our emotional health and well-being. We can't cut Hermes out altogether; that would be as unnatural as turning our backs on Hestia. We need communication; we need to let our minds expand outwards as much as we need them to expand upwards toward Helios, the sun. But just as we have to balance that upward striving with a remembrance of our earthly roots, we have to focus inward as well as out. Bringing Hestia back to her place in the heart of the house can start the healing process.

Above **In an ideal world, and an ideal home, Hestia and Hermes live in harmony. There is a fire in the grate, a sacred space for family mealtimes, and a feeling of peace and serenity that still allows a free exchange of ideas and influences from the outside world.**

HEALING HESTIA

There are plenty of simple ways of bringing Hestia back into the home. These are just some suggestions to start you off – once you remember the feeling of the goddess, you will undoubtedly find more ways of reintroducing Hestia yourself.

If you can have a living fire, then do so. There is nothing like sitting by a fire on a cold day, keeping warm and gazing into the flames. If you cannot have a real fire, there are now many beautiful gas fires which look realistic and give Hestia a symbolic home.

If all fires are out of the question, then buy a large scented altar or church candle, place it on a mantelpiece or table in the heart of the home and use that as the focus of your home. You could turn this space into a home altar by putting on it representations of you and your family: photos, anything symbolic or special; some fresh flowers; some incense. Light your candle every day for a short while and welcome Hestia into the flame and your home.

Hestia is the original housewife, in the sense of the word before it became so defamed. But there is no shame in caring for your home and keeping it clean and beautiful. Clean your home with care and pride (more on this in Part Three). Think of it as a kind of meditation; focus on what you are doing; be in the moment. Don't begrudge your time or look on your efforts as fruitless (dust arriving the moment you've dusted); use it as a time for reflection and centring.

Hestia loves the order of the home. Whether you live alone or share with hordes, make meal-times special and sacred by always sitting down to eat. Lay the table with care and put fresh flowers or something natural (beautiful pebbles, pots of herbs, unusual pieces of driftwood) as a centerpiece. Cook the food, however simple, with care and attention and serve it with love. Be conscious that you are not just feeding bodies but souls as well. Say grace before you eat, whatever your religious beliefs. It needn't be 'for what we are about to receive…', it could be a simple 'thank-you' to God, the Earth, the food, the cook. It might even be the old Roman 'To Vesta'.

One of Hestia's prime symbols is the circle, the ancient symbol of Mother Earth, of psychic wholeness, togetherness and unity. Anything that draws people together in the round is wonderful for connecting – think of Arthur's round table. It doesn't have to mean buying a new dining room table (although if you need one, maybe try thinking round!), but you could draw people around the fire or around a coffee table for drinks, around a picnic rug outside: when people are in a circle they automatically talk more and pay attention to each other.

Allow yourself a little Hestia time every day, a quiet time for pottering around your home, adjusting something here, moving something there. Give yourself a few moments to watch a shaft of sunlight glancing through a window. That chair looks inviting? Allow yourself some time to sit and muse. Day-dream.

Don't race, don't rush, don't try to do everything at once. Hestia is the goddess of focus. She teaches that we should become absorbed in one task at a time, working quietly and calmly with inward serenity. Her way may seem boring but it gets things done – efficiently and well.

If you are one of those madly sociable people who always has 'open house', make sure you have times when you or your family can be by yourselves. Explain that you might not always be available if people drop in – maybe you could have a sign to put up if you're in Hestia space, asking people to drop by another time? Explain to the kids that sometimes it's nice for you to eat together as a family – not just one or two of you and not with all their friends there either. Just the family. Hestia would like that.

Hestia can be brought into a room by the use of candles – representing the fire of the hearth, the placement of natural objects and a clean, calm feeling of order.

driving out hermes

Try cutting down Hermes' domination in your house.

- Move the television so it isn't the dominating center of the room. Then you won't be so likely to switch it on automatically when you come into the room.
- Try to cut down on newspapers and magazines. Do you need them all, every day?
- Do you have to listen to every news broadcast?
- Can you live a day or two without checking your e-mail?
- Can you switch on the answering machine and switch off your mobile once in a while and call people back in your time? Just be aware of how much you focus on Hermes and his toys.

the spirits of the home

do you believe a house possesses spirits or is it just superstitious nonsense? Most Westerners would agree that there are no such things as spirits of the house; guardians of the threshold; invisible entities which share our space. Yet this is the minority view. The vast number of non-Western cultures firmly believe in spirits: their homes are full of household gods, spirits and the souls of their ancestors. Their homes are alive, not just with the physical bodies of the humans who live in them, but with the energetic bodies of more ethereal creatures.

We may mock, but the same beliefs ran through our own cultures until not so long ago. Throughout Europe, houses had a veritable army of esoteric helpers: pixies and fairies; brownies and banniks. Early American settlers painted protective symbols on their houses and barns to keep away bad spirits; and put out a bowl of cream to attract the good.

SPIRITS AND SPRITES

Look through a book on the folklore of virtually any country and culture and the story is the same. In Scotland and parts of England there are brownies who attach themselves to a particular house and come out at night to perform the tasks that need doing – repairing, sweeping and protecting the livestock and family. In Wales there is the *pwca*, in Ireland the *puca* or *pooka*, in Denmark the *puge*. In the Baltic states a similar brownie-like figure is known as the *puk*. The names are almost identical and their functions are the same: to guard and help the household, providing the household respects and rewards them. Similar beings are the *shvod* of America, the *kikimora* of Russia, the *haltia* of Finland, the *befana* of Italy, the *nisse* of Scandinavia, the *nat* of Burma, the *phi* of Thailand. In Germany they are known as *kobolds* and will soothe the children of the house with sweet songs. In African folklore the protective spirits are *aiza*; in Lithuania the house spirits are *aitvaras* who appear as a cock inside the house and a fiery dragon outside.

Some spirits had specific tasks and places of abode – the *skritek* of Slavic lore dwelt behind the oven and was represented as a small boy, with his arms crossed and wearing a crown. His statue was placed on the hearth to guard the house when the family was not there. The *cluricaun* is an Irish spirit who lives in the wine cellar; in Germany he is known as the *biersal* and will keep everything spick-and-span – providing he is given a jug of beer every day. In Russia there is even the *bannik*, the spirit of the bathtub who needs to be placated by leaving a little water in the bath and some soap ready to hand, for him to use should the mood so take him.

All these folkloric spirits had features in common. They were tricky spirits, willing to help in whatever way they could – providing you earned their favor. If you did not appreciate them or failed to leave acceptable gifts (usually food or a bowl of milk) they would either fade away or plague the household with their mischief. They were shy beings, coming out only at night. And they were very proud. Virtually every custom says that, although you should show respect and gratitude, it should not be obvious. The reward should be left casually, as if by accident. And if you gave a brownie or one of his cousins a suit of clothes as a thank-you, you would never see him again. Peasant households took their spirits very seriously, leaving the best cakes and milk, in the kitchen. Farmers might also leave one cow unmilked, or let the first few drops of milk fall when they milked, as the fairies' rightful due.

Images of deities from many different traditions find a place in a home with true spirit. They are a symbolic reminder of the existence of unseen power.

HOUSEHOLD SPIRITS

In ancient Greece and Rome the home was packed full of gods, goddesses and a veritable army of household spirits. We have already met Hestia and Hermes but the Greeks would also honor Aphrodite in the home by introducing beauty and sensuality. In return she would endow the house with laughter, games, joy and peace. Hera was the goddess of marriage and she ruled over the formal areas of the house – the reception hall, the sitting room, the formal dining room: she expected visitors to be treated with due respect and honor. She revels in regular order and the smooth running of a house. In the ancient calendar the first day of every month, the Kalends, were dedicated to Hera. Little houses were made of clay as devotional objects sacred to her. Hestia was acknowledged every day but while she ruled the hearth, Demeter cooked on it – she bakes the bread and feeds the family. She is the great carer, the archetypal Mother. In the study, the library, the den you would find Athena, nose in a book. In a quiet space of her own, curled up on a window-seat or outside in a wild part of the garden you might catch Artemis.

In Roman households, Janus, the two-headed god, protected the gateway, the threshold to the house – looking both inward and outward, overseeing the family's coming and going and watching out for unwelcome intruders. Then there were two specific divisions of household spirit: the *lares* and the *penates*. The penates were worshipped alongside Vesta (Hestia) and were originally the gods of the storeroom. They were responsible for the household's food supply, and images of them, made of wax or ivory, were worshipped at shrines in the house. A fire was kept burning in their honor. The lares were originally considered to be the spirits of the ancestors. Head of the lares was the *lar familiaris*, the spirit of the founding ancestor of the family. Both lares and penates would receive worship and would be given offerings of food and wine in exchange for their role in protecting the house and family.

In China, the cult of dead ancestors was, and often still is, an essential part of life. Chinese homes have pictures of the ancestors and a little stove where they light incense at a kind of everyday shrine. Here they pray to their ancestors and remember them. In return the ancestors are thought to guard the house and bring luck and protection to those still living. There is a sense of continuation through the generations.

Left **Representations of the Christian saints and martyrs have long been a part of Roman Catholic homes, where color pictures of the crucifixion and statues of the cross often take pride of place in a room.**

THE RETURN OF THE SPIRITS

All very interesting, but all folklore and superstition, you might think. What relevance could these various spirits and gods possibly have for us today? Architect Christopher Day states categorically that every place should have its own living spirit, which can only be destroyed by brutal, unresponsive actions. Jungian analyst Marion Woodman agrees when she refers to the necessity of our recogniz-

Left **The gods, godesses and household spirits can be depicted in a number of different ways and in many different media. Contemporary interest in spirituality has made sacred objects from diverse cultures far more widely available.**

lar are very open to such spirits. They will spend hours looking for fairies at the bottom of the garden or chatting to 'friends' who, as they are invisible to us, we assume to be imaginary.

Lots of people swear they have seen spirits or ghosts in their houses. Sometimes these seem to be frightening but often they appear to be benign. Another common experience is that of seeing something 'out of the corner of your eye', often an animal-like shape. Spirits do not always take human form and many cultures believe in spirit animals as guardians and guides. The Roman genius of the place, another guardian spirit, was often portrayed as a serpent. In India, cobras are considered sacred and it's not uncommon for a family to live quite happily with a cobra in residence in the attic, protecting the house on a psychic level and keeping down the rats on the practical level.

Many people find the idea of a house filled with kindly spirits attractive. And it wouldn't take that much to bring them back to our consciousness. After all, we readily invoke Saint Christopher when we are going on a journey; we pray for our safety and well-being, to be kept safe through the night. It's only a small step further to imagine our houses filled with a whole host of guardian spirits. It doesn't matter whether you envisage them as pixies and lares or as angels or as gods. The important part is recognizing that the house is full of energetic forces as real as you are.

ing the intersection of the human and divine.

But what do we do in our houses? We may not be guilty of brutal actions, but certainly we're unresponsive to the spirits of our home. And we rarely allow even the possibility Marion Woodman begs, of a relationship between ourselves and the gods, spirits and energetic forces of the house. And yet, are our houses really completely empty of spirit life? Have the gods, angels and the household imps and sprites really abandoned us, sick of our neglect? Who can say? How often do you hear people complaining when they mislay things in the house that 'the poltergeist must have moved it' or the 'fairies have been here again'? Children, in particu-

Every place should have a spirit; indeed, unless it has been destroyed by brutal unresponsive actions, every place does.

Christopher Day, Architect

Older cultures always left room for the gods at the threshold and fireside, and in other parts of the home. If the possibility of the intersection of human and divine is recognized in daily life, then ritual does not seem foreign.

Marion Woodman, Jungian Analyst

THE HOUSE OF THE SPIRITS

Start to make room for the spirits by allowing yourself the thought that such things may be possible. Don't dismiss them out of hand. If you feel comfortable with the idea of sharing your home with unseen visitors, you could try some of the suggestions below. Remember that you can envisage these visitors in any shape you like: if you have a religious belief you may prefer to see them as angels or divine beings. If you feel happy with the classical archetypes, then the gods and goddesses of the home might feel more comfortable. If you're an earthy or pagan type you may revel in the idea of mischievous elemental beings and brownies.

In ancient Rome food that fell to the floor was at once considered to belong to the household spirits. Don't sweep it up immediately but give the spirits of the dead at least a while to take their fill before sweeping it up. Of course, if you have a dog (your very own Cerberus, mythological guard-dog of the underworld) you probably won't have to clean up at all.

If you like the idea of having your own brownie or spirit-helper, follow the age-old rules: leave out a saucer of milk or cream and maybe a couple of biscuits (many people retain this custom at Christmas, leaving mince pies and a glass of sherry out for Saint Nicholas, Father Christmas).

Find your own images to represent the lares and penates. Find a figure or image you like and tuck it away in a place from where it can look out over the house. It could be an angel, or a Hindu god or a good-luck piskie.

We'll meet Aphrodite, the goddess of beauty and love, in the following chapters, but evoke her blessing by making your house as beautiful as possible. Indulge her with fresh flowers (she is also goddess of flowers), a sumptuous cushion or sweet-smelling herb pillow; sweet scents and objects which please the eye.

Indulge Artemis by throwing open all the windows of your house when the fresh breezes of spring blow. She loves the open air and the call of the wild. She too will love flowers – particularly armfuls of blossom and wild flowers, even weeds. If you have an exercise bike or step, remember Artemis as you start your workout – she is the lean fleet goddess who can add a spring to your step.

Left **Isis is the Egyptian goddess of Earth and fertility. Mother of Horus, the sun god, she has held a position of spiritual importance for over 3,000 years.**

Remember your ancestors. In the

West we do precisely the opposite to the East. While Oriental people venerate their ancestors, we almost entirely forget them. Find photos of your ancestors if you can, as far back as you can. Frame them and display them in your house. You could follow the Chinese custom and set up an altar, with incense and a candle – see the chapters on feng shui for the best spots to place such an altar.

Above **Honor your ancestors by framing photographs of them and devoting one wall, or a homemade altar, to their memory.**

Read old folk tales and fairy stories and become familiar with the spirits of your culture and land. Better still, sit around the fire and read the stories out loud to your family or a group of friends. Share stories about your supernatural experiences and find out just how common they are. Everyone seems to know someone who's seen a ghost or 'felt' something strange.

Become sensitive to spots in your house which feel as if they might be home to the spirits. As we've seen, the threshold, the hearth, the larder, the bathroom, the cellar and attic are favorite spots.

Dogs were often considered guardian spirits of the threshold. If you can't have your own living guard-dog you might like to put a pair of guardian stone dogs (or lions or dragons) either side of your front door or in the inner hallway.

Some people feel their homes contain unpleasant spirits or ghosts which can make a house feel very uncomfortable. There is more about this in the section on space clearing.

psychology of the home

So far we have talked about the home in a mythological, archetypal and spiritual way. Now we should take some time to pull in from the wider picture and start to think about how our homes affect us in a more personal, psychological way. For our homes are reflections of our psyches – the home you pick and the way you choose to decorate it speaks reams about your psychological make-up; the way you view the world; your hopes and aspirations; your deepest insecurities and fears. By paying attention to the choices we make about our home, we can

start to understand more about our psyche and soul, just as we can by focusing on our dreams. Jungian psychologists believe that dreams are 'messages' or projections from the unconscious; within them are all the issues and unresolved business of our unconscious minds. By working with dreams we can often find answers to our most pressing dilemmas. In a similar way, we project our inner thoughts and preoccupations, our likes and dislikes, onto the fabric and furnishing of our homes. An adolescent may well leave his or her room in a mess as an unconscious gesture of defiance to the parents. Someone might buy a home that unconsciously emulates the style of the home of a much-loved, deceased relative, or rent an appartment which is a copy of a childhood home.

If you are a great hoarder of clutter, for instance, it could be because you are unconsciously trying to protect yourself against some possible lack in the future or that you are overly attached to the past and fear that the future cannot bring anything as valuable and meaningful as that which has gone before. Some people, however, are entirely the opposite. These are the ones who constantly make changes to their environment; who are always moving or always shifting the furniture. This could well point to a 'Peter Pan' complex: an unwillingness to ground oneself and to make commit-

ments; a perpetual unhappiness with the status quo. Of course, in an ideal world we would be somewhere in the middle – keeping a certain amount of our past with us, but also being confident of greeting the future too.

LEAVING HOME

Before we move on to what your present home says about you, think first of all about when you left home. Were you desperate to leave or was it a huge and hard wrench? Maybe you are still living at home. Some people find it almost impossible to leave home, even if they are fully grown and launched in life. Even if they do leave, they will try at all costs to re-create the childhood home. Jung explained this as a 'participation mystique' with the family in which they identify first and foremost as members of a family rather than individuals in their own right.

Not all 'stay at homes' have this participation mystique. Some suffer from 'eternal youth' syndrome – they can't seem to grow up and take on adult responsibilities. Usually this happens because they were so indulged as children that they just don't want to move from this cosy position. Or it might be because the underlying message they received from their parents was that being an adult was a

Above **For some of us, the artless display of clutter that we remember from our parents' home, in the days before fitted kitchens, can symbolize everything that we long for in our present houses. For others, the cluttered look will be an anathema.**

pretty miserable business and so it was better not to grow up at all.

Other people take precisely the opposite position. They can't wait to find their own home, to make their own choices. Sometimes this comes about from a basically unhappy childhood and a huge need to separate from the family and to make your adult life as different as possible. Such people will want to move far away, or choose a radically different style of house or furnishings from that of their parents. However, just because you raced away from home after leaving school and chose minimal rather than copying your parents' Victoriana, it doesn't necessarily mean you had an unhappy childhood. Some people live perfectly happy child-

hoods but grow up to lead very different lifestyles from those of their parents. Many people believe that these differences can be explained by Jung's system of typology.

> *'Participation mystique' affected some of my own relatives arriving as refugees from pogroms against the Jews. One woman continued to live with her parents even after she married. Her husband simply moved in; her own children grew up in that house; and she still lives there to this day. In the background there is obviously a great fear of any change, presumably because change has been associated with circumstances getting worse.*
>
> Sarah Dening, Psychologist

JUNG'S PERSONALITY TYPES

Jung believed that we could all be described by a system of four personality types and two modes of behavior. We are all familiar with the two modes: extrovert and introvert. But the personality types – thinking, feeling, sensation and intuition – are less well-known.

You probably already know if you are an introvert or an extrovert. The extrovert will always reach out towards the world; the introvert will instinctively draw back. Most people will fall cleanly into one or other camp. Of course, we all have times when we dip into the opposite (the extrovert who needs the odd patch of peace and quiet; the introvert who will suddenly become the life and soul of the party) but they are exceptions rather than the rule. When it comes to the home, extroverts tend to be concerned with how other people will regard their living space, and will often decorate and furnish the place with a view to entertaining, to impressing other people. Introverts, on the other hand, are more concerned with what feels comfortable for themselves. On the whole, interior designers tend to be extroverts!

When it comes to the four personality types, or 'functions' as Jung called them, it becomes a more subtle process. Jung realized that some people approached life predominantly by thinking while others dealt with life through their feelings. At first he thought that extroverts were the 'feeling' types while introverts would be thinkers but with time he realized it was more complex than that. Thinking and feeling were dimensions of personality quite independent of whether someone was extroverted or introverted. He also realized that there were two more functions – sensation, the information we receive through our senses of sight, hearing, taste, touch and scent; and intuition, the information we receive directly from the unconscious.

Each of us will tend to be a mixture of two or perhaps three reasonably well-developed functions with maybe one or two with which we do not identify. Let's have a closer look at each of the four functions and how they manifest themselves in the home environment:

Below **Without a speck of dirt anywhere or a thing out of place, this pristine kitchen could belong to a functionally minded sensation type or a feeling person: their homes tend to be rather sparsely decorated and 'unlived in'. Most likely the owner is a mixture of the two.**

SENSATION

People who have a strong sensation function are concerned above all with things as they are. They are less concerned with the aesthetics of the home than with whether or not an object is functional. If you are a sensation type, your home will run like clockwork! Shelves will go up, taps will not drip, painting will be done when necessary, curtains will be made with the minimum of fuss. You are concerned with how things are now, this moment, not next week or next year. Jobs get done because they need doing. You will always know the right place to go to get what is needed and your home will be in perfect order.

INTUITION

Intuitives are highly sensitive to atmosphere and the flow of energy. They are exactly the kind of people who would be drawn to feng shui, space cleansing – and to books like this! You can be the most original of all the types when it comes to creating an unusual and individual home. You may well create highly idiosyncratic surroundings, mixing styles, periods and influences. Practicality is not a major concern and your environment may well seem very eccentric to more design-conscious people. You are always on the look-out for possibilities. And while a kitchen, to the practical sensation type, is simply somewhere to cook, to the intuitive it could be anything – a studio, a conservatory full of plants, a mini temple – with the fridge and cooker hiding beneath greenery or drapes. Intuitives will make quite radical changes to their spaces and are not unduly concerned if this means having to get rid of perfectly serviceable items.

THINKING

If you have a strong thinking function you probably barely notice your surroundings at all. You are much more concerned with ideas than with things, and as long as you have somewhere to put your books and papers, you will be happy. Your house may well look chaotic to an outsider, but you know where everything is and will become quite upset if somebody comes along and tries to tidy you up. You really barely notice clutter building up and will have the most problem in the decluttering and clearing chapters of all the types. This is the archetype of the absent-minded professor with mouldy coffee cups all around the home.

Strong thinking types are not really interested in fads and fashions and so you will rarely make radical changes in the home, except maybe to upgrade the computer. You can be methodical

when you are sufficiently interested in something practical and are able to devote energy to it. However, it tends to be in response to something going wrong – maybe the bookshelves collapsing, for example. If someone comes along and shows you how much more comfortable you could be in your surroundings, you tend to be perfectly amazed.

Above **A thinking type is not interested in fads and fashions and only needs somewhere to put his or her books and papers.**

FEELING

Feeling is the opposite to thinking in Jung's system. The feeling type has very strong responses to everything in the home: style of house, furnishings, design, color, tone. You are the type of person most likely to call in an interior designer or to take great pains in designing your own home. Most likely you will want your home to feel good to others as well, so you go in for comfort – but always fashionable comfort. On the whole, feeling types have good, if somewhat conventional, tastes. Because you trust your feelings, you tend to be confident that others will find your home as beautiful and harmonious as you do yourself. You may well be offended if someone fails to appreciate what you have so carefully created.

Sometimes, however, the feeling person's home can be rather chilly: exquisitely appointed but somehow lacking a 'lived in' atmosphere. It could be the kind of place where you worry about dropping crumbs or marking the table.

Often a feeling person's home is filled with inherited items which don't really suit them. It seems surprising until you realize that the sentimental value is stronger than the aesthetic considerations.

UNDERSTANDING YOUR TYPE

Many people in therapy or analysis spend ages trying to decide which is their primary function, their secondary function and, perhaps most importantly, the inferior function (the function which is unconscious and often ignored). You will probably recognize yourself instantly, pinpointing either your primary function or gaining a strong feeling of your inferior function. In Jung's system, your inferior function is generally the opposite in a pair: thinking and feeling; sensation and intuition. So if you had a primary function of thinking, feeling would most likely be your inferior. The secondary functions would come from the other pair, that is, sensation and intuition. If your primary function were, say, intuition, then sensation would be your inferior function while you could back up your intuition with thinking and feeling.

Left **If you are most at home in the quiet and conventional surroundings of a library, with your nose in a book, then you are probably a classic thinking type who needs to get in touch with your feelings. If you are this type, trying a team sport will help you to relate to others.**

But why should it matter? Because by understanding your psychological profile you can learn your blind spots and also find yourself on a path to deeper self-knowledge and growth. The inferior function can be our weak point. While we use the other three functions more or less consciously, the inferior function is often, completely unconscious. You can see it in people who are primarily thinkers who totally deny all feeling; in intuitives who live in their heads, rather than in their senses. And vice versa. But while the inferior function can be our blind spot, it is also the source of great riches. By tapping into it we can access our unconscious, with all its vast potential for growth.

DEVELOPING THE INFERIOR FUNCTION

The following are some suggestions for getting in touch with your inferior function. They will most likely sound very unappealing or even distasteful. That's a good sign as it shows you have identified your weak spot. If you can bring yourself to develop this shadow side of your personality, you would almost certainly take a huge step forward in your Self development.

SENSATION

The world of sensation, the physical, the here and now, is a foreign realm for some people, particularly intuitives. And yet getting into the body can be enormously helpful. If sensation is your weak point, try practical activities which involve handling the shape and substance of things: pottery, gardening, dress-making, woodwork, DIY. Drawing or painting can be very useful. And any type of body-work, be it yoga, massage, Alexander technique, Rolfing or t'ai chi, would be superb.

FEELING

If you have a very pronounced thinking function then you could discover huge depths by allowing yourself to access the feeling side. The key is to find a way of relating to others while still maintaining clear boundaries. Working with a psychotherapist is an obvious starting point – group work would be particularly beneficial. You could join an evening class or find a team sport or other activity you might try. Dancing (line, folk or ballroom) would be ideal. Music can open the hearts of thinking types – so can keeping a pet. Working on your dreams in a dream group would be ideal.

INTUITION

Sensation types will just not understand the strange twilight world of the intuitive – they will probably dismiss it as complete nonsense. But daring to venture into the realm of intuition will bring remarkable results for sensates. Open yourself to the unknown by dabbling in oracles – try studying the *I Ching*, the runes or the tarot. Suspend disbelief for a while and see what happens. Learning to dowse would be an interesting activity – justify it by the fact that it's so practical and useful! You could also benefit greatly by working on your dreams – either alone or by joining a dream group.

THINKING

'I'm just not logical.' 'I rely on my feelings, not my rational mind.' Both classic comments from feeling types for whom the sane, logical function of thinking is a world away. Yet for a balanced psyche, feeling types need some processes which don't involve any emotional input. You'll turn up your nose but try getting into crosswords, puzzles and chess. If you're terrified of computers, challenge yourself to tap into the electronic world. A basic course in mathematics would be very positive. Try anything logic-based.

home as a reflection of soul

So by taking a good look at our homes, we can begin to understand more about ourselves. At the very least it can stop you beating yourself up because you simply can't seem to get to grips with a hammer and nails (of course you can't, you're an intuitive). It could create some understanding within the home – no wonder her room is so messy and cluttered, she's a typical thinker, her mind is on completely different things. However, it can go far deeper and become the start of a fascinating journey into the deeper reaches of the Self and into the soul itself.

By reordering our homes to reflect our souls truly and honestly, we can start the process of individuation, of becoming aware of who

we really are. We can begin to understand what is really important in our lives and what is just façade. We can come 'home' to a place inside ourselves where we feel natural, at peace. In this place we are not having to prove anything or be anyone other than who we truly are. Finding our true Self is the task we are all set in life – some people find it early; many only start the process in later life. But rethinking your exterior home is a vital part of the process. By understanding what is important and unimportant in the home environment we are putting up a mirror to our inner home, the soul.

When we start to listen to our souls we may find our outer homes need to change quite radically. We may realize we no longer want to be clinging to the past, holding onto the childhood home. Instead we want to choose our own pattern, our own life. We may realize that our home is too rational, too ordered and that our life reflects that perfect but static pattern. What we need is a little irrationality; something to kickstart a new phase in life. What better place to start than the home? When we want to bring something new into our lives, it's very common for us to change our job, finish a relationship or alter our image. Why not start instead by opting for a new color in the living room or a thorough decluttering session?

The following chapters look more deeply at our homes. We will start thinking about what, for us, constitutes the spirit of the home. Once we have our blueprint, our essential map, we will have discovered yet more about ourselves – and be well on the way to turning our homes into true havens for the soul.

Left **Think about the items you have around your home. Do they tell people anything about you? Is your décor quirky and playful, full of innovative ideas, or is it perfectly ordered and rational?**

Above **If you really want your home to reflect your true soul it must first be decluttered and, as far as possible, stripped bare. Then you can begin to introduce the elements that truly represent you.**

PART 2

thinking
about
home

returning home

now it's time to get down to some practical exercises. They are simple, fun to do and will enable us to discover what home really means to us and what we each want from our home of the spirit. First and foremost we need to realize that there is no one 'perfect' home. Each and every one of us has our own idea of the home of the soul. A country cottage is someone's dream but might be your nightmare if your ideal is an inner-city eyrie, a loft up among the rooftops. In order to find our spiritual homes we first need to do some homework. Most of us think we know exactly what we want; what we would buy if we won the lottery – but what our egos think we want and what our souls really crave are often two entirely different things. It takes some unearthing to find the true home of the soul.

The exercises which follow are designed to start you thinking. How much you get out of them is entirely up to you. You can flick through them and skim the surface – or you can take your time and really do some serious archaeology. If you decide to perform some solid digging, you will need a few tools.

WHAT YOU WILL NEED

First you will need to start collecting magazines. House magazines, lifestyle magazines, supplements. Most houses have a collection somewhere. If you're not a magazine reader, then see if your friends have any they can donate (don't ask for a loan; you will be cutting them up!).

You will also need two books. One should be about 8 x 12 inches, ideally with plain pages. Or a scrapbook would be fine. The other will be your journal so it can be any size – whichever you feel comfortable writing in. If you can, buy new books and choose ones which really inspire you. Finding your true home is a process of discovery, inspiration and enchantment so the books you use to chart your progress should fit the mood.

You will also need some colored pens or pencils – or paints. Plus some larger sheets of paper or an art pad.

If you have access to one, a tape recorder could be very useful. If there is someone you trust and feel comfortable with, a friend can be a great help with some of the exercises, writing down comments for you to discuss later.

Next, and almost most important of all, you need to give yourself a space and the time to get into the process. If you can, allow yourself at least a clear hour at a time to work on these exercises. Don't rush them. You will also need to hide away so you can concentrate without worrying about phones ringing or children crying. So pick your session times with care. Having said that, don't endlessly put it off if you never seem to be able to find the right time or place. It's better to snatch the odd moment here and there than not do it at all. Many people find that their best thoughts come at unexpected moments – lying in bed, last thing at night, just about to doze off to sleep, for instance, or when musing over a cup of coffee. So really there's no prescription – do it whichever way feels best for you.

PREPARATIONS

Each time you begin working on your soul home it is a good idea (although not essential) to work through these preparations. They serve to focus your intent and put all your resources, both conscious and subconscious, at your service. They also mark the transition between your everyday world and this process.

Find somewhere quiet where you won't be disturbed. You might like to light a candle or maybe burn some incense, or put some aro-

A modern, open-plan apartment offers plenty of scope for spacious, gracious living. The use of glass partitioning helps to break down the distinction between outdoors and in.

trying to tell you. It's not unlikely that some part of you may be unwilling or uneasy about this process.

Sometimes when people think deeply about home, they discover that they need to make deep changes – not just moving the furniture but shifting something deep within. Perhaps at some level you may be aware of this and part of you is scared or unwilling to change. That's fine – just be aware of it and comfort yourself by reminding yourself that you always have a choice. Nothing will be forced upon you. Nothing will be changed unless you really want it so.

matherapy oil into a burner. If you have a lar, or spirit of the house, you may want to put his or her image on the table in front of you too.

If you find a feeling of resistance in any part of your body after doing the exercises in the box (right), just be aware of it and anything it may be

relaxing and centring yourself

- Give yourself a good stretch. Reach right up to the ceiling, as if trying to touch the stars. Feel yourself pulling out of your waist and the stretch running right up through your back, shoulders, neck and into your head.
- Now let your body slump forwards, letting your head dangle down and your hands reach toward the floor. Go as far as you feel comfortable.
- Now roll your head slowly and carefully from side to side, feeling the stretch in your neck tendons. Now rotate your head right round clockwise and then anticlockwise. Shake out your entire body.
- Lie down on the floor and stretch out again, as long as you can. Now bring your knees up toward your chin and let them fall to the right while your head and shoulders twist over to the left. You may feel your vertebrae crunching a little.
- Repeat on the other side. Now you should feel physically more comfortable. NOTE: If you have any back or neck problems, or any form of arthritic condition, check with your physician before stretching.
- Ask for a blessing on your work. You could ask for the guidance of your guardian angel or the angel of the house. Or perhaps dedicate your efforts to Hestia, guardian of the home. Or just spend a few moments in silence, meditating. Whichever you choose, you are simply clearing your mind and offering your subconscious the opportunity to relax and support you.
- Spend a few minutes softly following your breathing, becoming aware of your lungs and your heartbeat. Be centered in your body. Is there any tension left in any part of your body? If so, try to relax it and let it go.

your first home

One slight word of warning before you begin the process of revisiting your first home. Most people will find no problem at all with these exercises – they will simply be fun and, it is hoped, very illuminating. However, it may be that your early experiences of home were not happy and that revisiting them could cause painful thoughts and memories to resurface. If you know you had an unhappy childhood or suspect you might have done, it would be advisable for you to work through these exercises with a trained psychotherapist or hypnotherapist.

Equally if, when you start working this way, you find that uncomfortable feelings or memories emerge, you should find a qualified professional whom you trust and talk through what comes up.

As we've already discussed, your childhood home can have an enormous effect on your entire life – particularly on your attitude toward home. So we'll start right at the beginning.

A JOURNEY THROUGH TIME

We're going on a journey back in time. It should last as long as you feel comfortable with it, but no longer than 20 minutes. Our first port of call is to the most important home of your childhood. This may be your very first home; at least the first one you can remember – or it could be the one in which you spent the most time as a child. You should choose the house that was the 'major' home of your young years. This first exercise will put you into a state of deep relaxation. If you don't feel comfortable with this, you can adapt the exercise by cutting out the instructions for going down the flight of stairs and simply using your memory and imagination in a full state of consciousness.

If you are fully awake you can note down your thoughts and feelings in your journal as you go along. If you are keeping your eyes closed you may find it helpful to use a tape recorder, or have a friend ask you the questions and note your responses. If you would like, you can take your guardian angel or spirit with you on your journey.

Settle back and make yourself comfortable. Close your eyes and focus again on your breathing. Breathe softly but deeply, gently slowing down your breathing to a comfortable rhythm. Check through your body to make sure you are as relaxed as possible. Now imagine you are standing in front of a short flight of stairs. You are going to walk down the stairs, one at a time, counting slowly from one to ten. As you walk you are aware that you are going down deeper into the past, down into your childhood, down to the house you used to live in, down, down and down. Count each step as you go, reminding yourself, 'one, going down,' 'two, going deeper down'…until you are right deep down at ten. Before you is a door. The door looks familiar because it is the front door of your first real home. Look at the door and recognize it – the color, the material, the knocker, maybe the number? Slowly the door opens and you walk through.

You are now in your childhood home. Is it the one you were expecting or somewhere else? Take your time to get your bearings. The front door is behind you so now look and see what lies ahead. Walk around. Go into every room and remember what it was like: how was it decorated? What colors were there? What was the furniture like? What could you see out of the window? What did you do in that room? Was it one you went into often or rarely, or not at all? Who used that room? What was the feeling of the room? Did you feel safe here? Go round the whole place like this, remembering, recording. You will find you remember extraordinary details about this home – details you had quite forgotten.

Where were your special places in the house? Where was your bedroom and what was it like? See yourself in your room – what are you doing? Did you have a special place to play, to read, to dream? Was it a secret place, a corner? Where was it? See yourself there. How old are you at this time? Are you happy, content? What are you doing; how do you feel?

Certain objects remembered from childhood may have a special resonance for you today without you quite understanding why. It is possible that you are attempting to recreate aspects of your childhood home in the house you have now, on a subconscious level.

Where was the heart of your home? Which room or part of a room encapsulated the soul of the house? Stand there and wait a moment while you connect to how you feel. What are your feelings towards this place? What emotions does it raise? Were you happy there?

Can you connect with the spirit of that house? What is it/he/she like? How did the house feel about your family? Ask the spirit of the house for the house's impressions of your time there. Ask the spirit for any useful insights into this early house. What key words would you use to describe this house? What color do you associate with it? What smell or scent? What name would you give the house to sum up your feelings about it?

Are there any elements of this childhood home which make you feel nostalgic? Is there anything there you would love to incorporate into your present home – whether something in the physical structure, the furniture or furnishings or a feeling or mood? Is there anything you dislike, which makes you feel uncomfortable? What don't you like about the house?

This is quite enough for your first trip back in time so say goodbye to the house and thank the spirit of the house for helping you. Make your way back to the front door and gently open it. Before you is the short flight of steps, as before. Step out and start walking up to the first one as the door closes gently behind you. Count from ten to one as you go up the steps, up towards a light which you know is your home in the here and now. As you go up you feel yourself becoming more and more awake, more and more aware of the world around you. You are feeling relaxed and yet full of energy. Up and up, more and more aware, hearing the everyday noises around you, feeling your weight, sitting on the chair. One – and you're back in your room, fully awake, fully aware. Open your eyes and stretch.

Spend some time thinking about what you saw, heard, smelt, and felt. Record it all in your journal as soon as you can, while it is still clear in your mind. Or, if you have a friend with you, you could talk it over with them, and then make notes in your journal. Were there any surprises?

REVISITING HOME

Now you know this process you can use it whenever you want to revisit your childhood home to find out more information. Remember always to record your observations.

As you become used to the process you might like to ask yourself and the house some extra questions:

- If you were old enough, did your friends come round to play at your house? Or did you spend most of your time at their houses? If so, why?
- Were there any rooms you don't remember? Do you know why?
- Did you ever have nightmares? Did you ever see anything strange – spirits, ghosts?
- Were you able to be on your own or did you have to share space with others most of the time?
- Was your home a happy place for children? Were you able to play and be yourself or did you have to be 'careful of the furniture'?
- Were you forbidden to touch certain things or to go into certain rooms?
- What features of the house or objects in it fascinated you? Can you remember ornaments?
- Try to recall key pieces of furniture. The table you ate on, the cooker, the sofa, the television, your bed, the bath, anything else. Which were the most important objects in your home?

Finally, to complete the picture, think about the other places of your childhood. Were there any houses you really loved? Whom did they belong to (grandparents, friends, neighbors)? What did you love about them? What particular aspects drew you to them?

DRAWING HOME

Now you have a pretty full picture of your childhood home. But to make it even more complete, use your subconscious in a different way. Take out a piece of plain paper and spread it out in front of you. Lay out your colored pens, paints or crayons. Now draw or paint your home in whatever way you like. Let your intuition guide you: pick up the colors that feel right, use whatever method you choose. It doesn't have to be a graphic representation – it could be simply colors and shapes. You could try representing the outside of the house, an interior or simply the mood of the house.

Do as many paintings or drawings as you like. What do you notice about them? Are the colors bright, pastel or dark? Do you use soft, rounded shapes and edges or harsh, blunt ones? What feelings do your pictures arouse in you? If you can't understand your painting, try talking to it. Imagine it can answer your questions and put questions back to you. This isn't madness; it's a recognized technique in art therapy and may give you some surprising insights. Now draw the spirit of your house. What is it/he/she saying to you?

You can also write to your painting – or write down a dialogue between yourself and the spirit of the house. Paste all your paintings and thoughts in your journal. If they are too large, keep a special folder or place for them.

Below and right **Try to capture the essence of your childhood home. Visualize the special way the light came into the room, the smell of fresh flowers in a vase, the way a cushion lay across a chair.**

MOVING ON

These techniques do take time but, if you find them enjoyable, it would be really useful to apply them to the other places you have lived in, before you moved to your present home. Or maybe there was a particular home which sticks in your mind as important: it would certainly be worthwhile going through the whole process on that place. If you don't have the time or the inclination then spend some time thinking about the following and record your answers in your journal:

- Have you lived in very similar places throughout your life or have they differed widely?
- Which was your happiest home? Why do you think that was? What elements of it made you feel good? Spend more time with this place – perhaps going through the early exercises or painting the home.
- Did you spend long periods away from your early homes? Were you sent away to school or to camp or to stay with relatives? Did you enjoy going away and, if so, what did you particularly like about it? Did you look forward to going home? What did you particularly miss about home?
- What was your first home of your own? Was it when you went away to a new job or when you went to school or college? What was it like? How did you make it your own? Did it feel good to be in your own place or did you miss your old home?
- As you grew up and moved out of your family home, did you have to share your space? Did you have room-mates? Did you enjoy sharing with other people or did you crave your own company?

These exercises build up a kind of web. At first they may not seem to make sense but as you constantly add to them and review your thoughts, you will most probably see a clear pattern. Certain thoughts, moods, ideas, feelings will repeat over and over again: watch out for these markers of the soul.

PINPOINTING THE FEELING OF HOME

For this exercise you will need to enlist the help of a friend. It would also be very useful to record your answers. Make sure you're comfortable and relaxed before you start. Basically, you are going to have your friend ask you a series of questions. You simply answer – don't try to think deeply about your answers or censor yourself, simply be honest. Don't worry if your answers don't seem to relate directly to home – they may not. Your friend needs to be listening out for any words which you appear to emphasize or which you repeat a lot. Listening in this way is quite an art so the tape recorder could be useful. Also it will enable you to hear your own emphases – we rarely detect them while we're speaking. So here are the questions:

- Remember a time in childhood when you felt totally happy and content. Where were you? What were you doing? What made it special? How did you feel? Were you by yourself or with anyone else? Which aspect of the memory did you enjoy the most?
- Think of a good time in your adolescence. Ask the same questions as in question one.
- Capture a moment when you felt most yourself, most complete, at home. Where were you? What were you doing? Again, ask the same questions as before.
- Think about a favorite hobby or pastime – in the past or present. Explore this in the same way.

As you were describing these times you will have emphasized particular words and phrases – write them down on a piece of paper and look for the patterns. Which keep recurring? Which represent important values or feelings for you? If you could only choose three or four of these phrases or words what would they be? What do they tell you about what makes you feel good in life?

You may find your answers don't seem to refer to home at all: you might have words and phrases like 'laughing with my friends' or 'exploring my spirituality' or 'respect'. But think deeply: this exercise roots out what is most important in your life – the values and feelings that make you feel comfortable and at home in the world. You may need to feel free and without ties; you might like the company of people; you may feel it's important above all to devote time to spiritual concerns; you may feel work is the most important aspect of your life; you may crave power and respect. All of these issues affect your requirements from your home. Your home can support you in every part of your life if you let it. But you do need to know what you want.

PUTTING IT TOGETHER

You should now have a huge amount of information, very important information. Take a little time before we move on to look at it all and see if you can see any patterns emerging. As you look back over the homes you have lived in, are there any similarities? Can you see any themes running through them? They might have been in very different locations and be different architecturally, but were there any elements in common? Did they all have high ceilings perhaps?

Or a similar atmosphere? Were they all messy or super-clean?

Above all, what were the elements of those early homes that you have carried with you? Do you pick similar homes for yourself? Or are you still rebelling against your parents? Are there any elements of your early homes that you miss and would love to re-create? What words sum up those early ideal aspects of home? If your home was not a happy place, what are the words that sum up what you dislike about home? Would the opposite word adequately describe what you are looking for now? In other words if your early homes were cold, do you crave warmth? If there was constant noise and activity, do you yearn for silence and peace? If you were left alone, do you want company, fun and laughter? Start looking for connections, for key words, for moods, atmospheres, feelings, colors, smells, the feel of things. You're weaving a tapestry of your ideal soul home.

The way we felt about our childhood homes provides the blueprint for what we will look for in all our homes to come.

your ideal home

You've already done a lot of the groundwork, the really hard graft. Now the fun begins. By this stage you should have quite a clear idea about the factors that influenced your early experience of home. You know which elements you want to reproduce in your home and those you don't want to include. Now let's start thinking about your soul home. This is not a time for reality so you can push to one side the little nagging voice that says 'but you're not a millionaire so you can't have your perfect home'. Or 'you don't deserve a soul home'. Or even

'you're wasting your time'. For the moment, we're going to indulge in pure imagination, pure wish-fulfilment. While you carry out the exercises in this chapter, forget for a while that you may share your home with others; don't think about their needs for the time being. Just focus on you and what your soul craves.

to which you're drawn. Don't be too picky at this stage, simply snip or tear out the ones you like. They might be exteriors or interior shots of houses. They could be colors, textures or objects. Equally, they might be lifestyle shots – people relaxing, laughing, working,

STARTING YOUR IDEAL HOME FILE

Now's the time to get out that cache of magazines and supplements. Sit yourself down in a comfortable armchair. Perhaps you might put on some of your favorite music, something inspiring, the kind of music you would play in your ideal home. Spend a few moments centring yourself – if you feel like doing the preparatory exercises in the previous section, so much the better – you will feel more relaxed and comfortable. Provide yourself with a good warming or cooling drink (depending on the weather, it might be a warming mug of coffee or herbal tea, or a long cool juice or soda). If it's the evening you might settle down with a good bottle of wine or a comforting snifter of brandy. Whatever. Cookies, nuts, a box of chocolates too. Why not? This should be fun.

Now start to flick through your first magazine. You're looking out for any pictures that grab your attention,

Right **This smart, solid-looking traditional structure with its gleaming white paint and pots of bright spring flowers would be an ideal home for many people.**

exercising, walking in the country-side, sitting outside a city café. They could be symbols, abstract pictures which sum up a feeling; words and phrases which strike a chord. The only criteria are that they make you feel good.

Go through all your magazines until you have a large pile of snipped pictures. Depending on the amount you have collected, this may take several sittings. You might need to do it over a period of time if you are short on magazines. If this is the case, consider asking friends and family for their old ones; or beg some from your doctor or dentist (ask for the dog-eared ones – it doesn't matter to you what they look like; you only want the pictures).

Put all your pictures in a folder and put them to one side. You will need to wait a day or two so the next time you see the pictures you are doing so with a fresh eye. The next step is sorting them out. This time you are looking for the pictures you really adore, that represent your ideal home for you. Look at each picture and ask yourself: 'Would I want to live here?' 'Does this sum up the feeling of home I really want?' If so, put it on one pile; if not, put it on another. You can always go back to your 'dump' pile and reconsider.

Now get out your plain journal, some scissors and paper glue (use paper glue because if you want to take pictures out at any point they can be removed easily instead of ripping both pictures and journal). You're ready to start putting together a picture of your perfect soul home. We are using pictures because they speak directly to the unconscious. When you look at a picture you generally know instantly whether you like it or not – although you might not know why. Working this way you could find out some surprising things about what your soul really wants from your ideal home.

Pause before you put a picture in your book. This book will be the story of your home, and using pictures in this way can have the curious effect of making your dreams come true. So be careful what you wish for! You are, in effect, programming your unconscious to make your dreams come true so think carefully about each picture. Is it really what you want? Listen to your heart. If so, if it is absolutely right (or if the essence is right), then cut it out neatly and stick it in. Continue through your 'yes' pile in the same way. You don't have to fill the whole book at once – you may well

Right **An immaculate state-of-the-art purpose-built apartment where the light streams in through glass ceilings and there's plenty of room for a grand piano might be exactly what your soul craves.**

want to add pictures as you go through this process. Equally you may well find, as you flip through, that certain pictures jar or just don't feel right. Fine, just take them out and add something else.

Look through your book often – every day at the beginning – and see what patterns are emerging. You may be surprised at how different your pictures are from the house you live in, the home you may have thought was your ideal.

use your senses

t his pictorial journal is a very visual exercise and, if you don't consider yourself a visual person, you might find it less satisfying. But do still give it a go, even if you only find a handful of pictures. However, you also need to use your other senses to find your ideal home. For these exercises, do go through the preliminary procedures described earlier in order to put yourself into a nice relaxed day-dreaming state of mind. Then let your imagination have full rein and you will be ready to embark on an intoxicating journey through the realms of the senses.

SOUND

Think about the sounds you want in your home. Imagine you were having breakfast in your ideal home: would you hear birdsong or the horns of early traffic? Would you be listening to the early news on the television or would there be Gregorian chant fluting through the space? How about when you come into the home – do you want to be greeted by a deep welcoming silence or the hubbub of voices? Will a cat stroll out to wind himself around your legs, meowing you home, or will a child hurl herself into your arms, regaling you with tales of her day? Will you greet your partner with a kiss or hug yourself with pleasure at the peace of your own space? How about when you fall asleep at night? What are the sounds you want to hear – both in and outside your own space?

Will you have a good-quality sound system? In what rooms of the house? Will you have a television and where? Telephones and fax machine – in which room or rooms? Do you like the sound of the telephone ringing or does it fill you with dread? Will you install an answering machine and keep the phone silent sometimes? Do you like the sound of neighbors around you or does it drive you mad? Do you like to hear other people moving around your home – or not? How important are the sounds of nature? And the sounds of society? Many people think they crave the 'silence' of the country but actually feel uneasy without the comforting noises of life around them. And remember that the countryside is not always quiet: people who are unused to it often complain about the cows keeping them awake or that the foxes screaming wake them up in terror. Write down your preferences in a page or two of your journal under the heading 'THE SOUNDS OF HOME'.

SMELL

Don't ever underestimate the sense of smell. It can make a home feel welcoming or push you out more quickly than almost anything else. What are the scents and smells of your ideal home? Sure, there are flowers, oils and perfumes, but think about more subtle smells. Do you love the fresh ozone of the ocean or the scent of pine from a forest? Or do you really feel at home with the smells of the city – the millions of scents which make up its ever-shifting perfume? Can you remember scents from the past that you love: the comfort of freshly laundered linen; the lavender in your mother's furniture polish; creosote on the garden fence; freshly brewed coffee; Sunday roast; a bubbling stew?

Think, too, of the smells you dislike – both from the past and the present. Many people hate the smell of damp, of petrol or of modern paints. Bathroom cleaner can be a big turn-off. The smell of dust is unpleasant and gives many people sneezing fits.

Again, put down your thoughts in a page or two of your journal under the heading 'THE SCENTS OF HOME'

Vibrant colors, a jug of fresh flowers and a platter of tangy-scented citrus fruit, plus the use of natural wood make this room a haven for the senses.

TOUCH

If we often forget about smell, we usually ignore touch altogether. Yet how our homes feel to the touch is so important. Once again, think about the textures you love, what feels good against the skin. Go back to the past – the cosy flannel sheets your grandmother used to put on the beds in winter; the tatty sheepskin rug you fell in love with; the soft velvets and furs you used to brush past in department stores (when you were too little to know about the cruelty of the fur trade). Nowadays you probably still love all those feelings but would add some more. There is nothing to beat the utterly fresh clean linen of a good hotel, the smooth feel of polished wood under foot but also the rough texture of natural matting such as coir and sisal. Velvet still entices; but so does corduroy, satin, silk and pure new wool. The silky feel of a bath with added oils and unguents; the smoothness of a sea-battered stone; the curves of a piece of skilfully turned wood; the soft hair of a ripe peach.

On the other hand, there are plenty of unpleasant sensations most of us would rather avoid: nylon sheets for one. Synthetic carpets; vinyl wallpaper; plastic furniture which leaves you all sticky and sweaty. Work out those sensations you like and don't like and once again put them in your journal under THE FEELINGS OF HOME'.

TASTE

Your soul home should offer the possibilities of delicious tastes too. Scent and texture play a large part here: the aroma of freshly ground coffee or baking bread whets the taste buds. So, too, does a bowl of luscious fruit or a plate of chestnuts waiting to be roasted on the fire.

Think of your favorite tastes and how you'd like to enjoy them in ideal surroundings, in your soul home. You might have your favorite croissants with home-made preserves for breakfast; imagine lunchtime picnics (sitting either on a freshly mown lawn or on a thick rug in front of a roaring fire on the living room floor); candlelit dinners or late-night toast and cocoa. These are also important. So add them to your journal under the heading 'THE TASTES OF HOME'.

The cool, smooth feel of fresh, clean bedlinen against your skin is one of the best sensations there can be, especially on a hot and humid night in the middle of a heatwave.

Never forget the glorious sense of touch: contrast the soft smoothness of a velvet cushion with the rough, hairy texture of natural matting such as coir or sisal.

thoughts from abroad

While you were pulling out pictures for your journal you may have been drawn to homes from other countries around the world. They may be places you have never set foot in; or you may remember with a sneaking fondness spots you stayed in on vacations or trips. Spend a little while recalling those places. Try to think what it is about these places which is so attractive to your soul. It might be the pure simplicity of a white-washed Greek house. The earthy comfort of a Spanish hacienda. The sugar-candy colors of the Caribbean.

The exotic textiles and statues of India and the Far East. The resinous wood of a Tyrolean cabin. The rough-hewn rock of a Scottish croft.

What was the feeling of these places? How did they achieve their atmosphere? Is there anything you could take out of those places – maybe a color scheme or furniture or simply a way of managing space, of arranging the atmosphere? Add these thoughts to your journal.

YOUR LIFESTYLE

Who are you? What are your roles in life and how do you play them? Your home should reflect all the important aspects of your life, but often we don't even know what these aspects are, so spend a little time thinking about the roles you play. You may be thinking, 'I don't play roles; I'm just me', but that's not true for most of us. You might well be computer analyst, daughter, aunt, mother, wife, friend. And that's just for starters. Think more deeply and you might also be quilt-maker, horse-rider, poet, hermit, life and soul of the party, wonder-cook, and red-hot lover.

Write down all your roles in life – first of all, list all the ones you play out now. Draw a circle and divide it into segments indicating how much time you devote to each role.

This exercise can be a real eye-opener and it can show you the areas of your life that your soul is missing. Once you see a graphic representation of your life in this way, it may push you to make some changes. After all, as has been noted so many times, whoever regrets on their death bed not having done more overtime? None of us knows how much time we have left on this earth, so perhaps we should live our lives the way we want them – now. Of course, we have to earn our living but there are ways of fitting in the other things, the important things, too.

So now draw another wheel and divide that in a different way: giving adequate amounts of time to each role. You might be someone who has devoted her life to her roles as mother, carer, daughter, wife, family taxi service, cook, washerwoman, cleaner, understanding confidante. You might be dying to get out there into the world and be also a go-getter, money-spinner, executive, business-owner. You might even be desperate to break free of your home in any way you can. Fine. Believe it or not, your home can help you in this too. At this point, though, just be clear about what you do want. Would you like to spend all your time out of the house? Or just have a better balance?

Whatever roles you want to play more of, your home can help you. It doesn't matter how small or cramped it is; you can always find a way of pursuing your goals. We'll look at these as we go through the book. For now it's enough that you've planted the seed, you've set your unconscious to work on the issue. You may find answers sooner than you expect.

Filling your home with artefacts from other countries and cultures can help you to recreate something of a place you remember with fondness.

BRINGING IT ALL TOGETHER

By now you will have a huge amount of information in both of your journals. It's time to start bringing it all together, thinking and feeling what a soul home really means to you.

You will no doubt have realized that a soul home is not something totally out of reach, down Millionaires' Boulevard. It's quite likely that your own home just needs a few adjustments to fill your soul quite nicely. These final exercises will focus your thoughts and let you see what needs to be done.

PAINTING HOME

Firstly, get out your paints again. Draw or paint a picture of your ideal home. As before, it doesn't need to be a perfect representation; it just needs to be meaningful for you. You might also write down your thoughts – as straight text or maybe a poem. It doesn't

matter which – just encapsulate all your feelings of home in your writing or drawing. As you draw or write, run these thoughts through your mind:

- What are the most important aspects of home?
- What feeling would you like as you walk through your front door?
- What words summon up home for you? What are the principal images, scents, sounds, feelings?
- What roles do you want to play in your home? What words sum up those roles?
- What is the most important piece of furniture in your house? Why? Which are your next three most important pieces?
- If you had to leave your home in an instant and could take only six items, which would they be? What if it could be only one? (Let's assume that all the humans and animals are quite safe for this exercise!)

If your home were a color, which would it be? If it were a shape, what would that be? If it were a symbol…? If it had a secret name…?

THE TREASURE MAP

Now we're going to get out the magazines again and our journal with the pictures. You will also need a large sheet of paper – maybe 16 x 24 inches, although it could be smaller (it depends on the size of your pictures). We're going to put together a treasure map. This is one of the most powerful techniques there is. Basically, you are programming your unconscious to manifest something for you. By putting a clear representation of your desires and intentions in graphic form, things somehow just start to happen. It could be the ultimate form of synchronicity, the moving of the Tao, quantum physics in motion …maybe a combination of all those things.

You can use the treasure map technique for any part of your life but at this point we're using it to attract the soul into our home. So start picking out the pictures which embody the 'feel' of home. They may not be specific – but they could well show the colors, moods and feelings of your soul home. Paint your piece of paper a color which embodies your perfect home. If you're not sure, paint it gold, which attracts good things to you, or a soft golden pink. Now paste on the pictures, making sure they really do represent your soul home. Add pictures that show the roles you want to play in your home. Leave a gap in the middle and paste on a photograph of yourself. You may also like to include words and poems – but make sure the main emphasis is the pictures.

Now pin up your picture in a place where you will see it every day. Maybe in the kitchen or by your desk. If you find it embarrassing, put it in a drawer you open frequently. Every time you look at it, imagine your house becoming full of the sense and soul in your map. Now let the map do its work…

Left **It may be that your present home only needs a few small adjustments to turn it into your true soul home: a place filled with warmth, color, texture, delicious aromas and other sensual delights, where Hestia rules supreme.**

Above **Once you have finally recognized what you really want from your soul home, you can start to create it. You may find that using the treasure map helps you to speed up this process.**

the miracle question

how are you feeling after all this work? Excited and energized or a bit flat and hopeless? Often our dreams can seem impossible, and it can almost feel unfair to dream and imagine because you can never envisage those dreams coming true. By now you might be thinking that this process is fine if you have a good income or the prospect of moving. But what if you're broke; what if there is no way out of your present home and situation? That can feel tough. But, it could be that you don't really need to move – you just need to shift your

perspective. It may sound trite to say that money doesn't buy happiness, but newspaper reports show that the majority of lottery winners are not happier afterwards; in fact, the money often causes anguish. Or think of the celebrities who find only loneliness in their wealth.

If you're still not convinced, ask yourself the Miracle Question. It is adapted from a technique used in Solution Focused Therapy, a highly effective model of psychotherapy. If you really spend some time on this, you may find out some astounding things. The questions are simple, but they focus on your behavior – something you have the power to change – rather than externals such as money. So, say you did win the lottery, or move to a beautiful big house. How would you behave? You might be more relaxed, happier, more peaceful. How would your family know? You might play with the children more; call up your parents to chat; be less irritable. Get the idea? Now, those are all things you could alter without winning the lottery.

You can use the Miracle Question specifically about your home. How would you know you had your soul home? How would you behave in it? How would your family behave? Try it and you may find that many of the qualities of your soul home are not dependent on the physical structure of the house but on your mood and actions. Change those and any humble abode can become a dream home.

Opposite **Winning the lottery might enable you to buy a beautiful big house, complete with chandelier, but would you really be happy? No amount of money can help you to put the soul back into your home if it is absent.**

the miracle question

Ask yourself the following questions:
- If you woke up and all your problems had disappeared, how would you know a miracle had happened?
- How would you behave differently? (Be as precise and exact as possible.)
- How would your family and friends behave differently? How would they know a miracle had happened? How would they see the differences in your behavior?
- Are there parts of the miracle that are already happening in your life?
- How have you got these things to happen? Can you get more of them to happen?
- What elements of your life at present would you like to continue?
- On a scale of nought to ten (where nought is the worst your life has been and ten is the day after the miracle), where are you now?
- If you are on, say, four, how would you get to five? What would you be doing differently?
- How would your family and friends know you had moved up one point?

a tour of your home

So far we've been living in our heads, indulging our imagination, letting loose our unconscious to play with the idea of home. Now it's time to get back to the real world and look at your actual space, the home you live in now. It may be that all the work you have done will end up by manifesting a totally new home for you (it does happen) but don't rely on it. For now you already have a home and one which most likely needs attention. Even if you are not going to remain in your home you owe it to the place, and to the people who come after you, to put back its

soul. So let's begin. Walk outside your home (you may like to take a notebook or your tape recorder with you). Imagine that you are seeing the house or apartment block for the very first time – as if you were a complete stranger, maybe a prospective buyer coming to view the place. First of all look at the front door, the entrance. What impression does it give? Is it welcoming or off-putting? You may live in an area where your entrance needs strong security – if so, does this give the place a sense of comforting protection or of a prison? These are subtle differences but they matter. Open your front door – does it open easily or stick? You need to be able to enter smoothly into your home – a sticking door will make you feel irritable before you even enter your space.

Now you're in the hall, or maybe the front door leads directly into one of the rooms. Is there a transition place? Some way of marking that you have come from outside to inside? In ancient Greece and Rome the hallway was considered a place between the two worlds, outside and inside, protected by Hermes/Hestia and the two-headed Janus. Is there somewhere to wipe your feet, to hang a coat maybe or to take off your shoes? You need to be able to pause on the threshold, to adjust to moving from one area to another.

Notice the smell of the house. Is it fresh, clean and welcoming or is it stale and musty? Our noses are so

Take time to pause on the threshold or landing. Does your home smell clean? If not, open the windows for at least 20 minutes a day and invest in some pots of sweet-smelling herbs.

sensitive they pick up the slightest scent. Making your home smell fresh requires more than a quick spray of air freshener – it takes deep cleaning (more in the next chapters).

Look around your home from this first vantage point. What does it say about the people who live here? Don't worry about whether it looks like a show home or is immaculately tidy – just think about the impression you get. Is it a bustling family home? A smart, maybe a little clinical, abode of a hard-working executive? Is it

full of character, if a trifle cluttered, or is it bare and faceless? Does it welcome you in or keep you at arm's length? Does it make you smile or make you want to turn around and walk straight out again?

Continue your tour into every room of the house, spending time thinking about each one: what's your first impression; what do you see, smell, hear? Does it serve its purpose? In other words, does your kitchen entice you to start making memorable meals – either for yourself or others? Does the bedroom call you to wrap yourself in sweet slumber? Does your bathroom beckon as a pleasant place to bathe and pamper your body? Are children's bedrooms safe, comforting places? Are teenagers' spaces fun, stimulating and exciting? Is your living room the kind of place that just begs for gatherings of people, laughter, good conversation? Is there a place you can sit quietly and muse, maybe gazing out of a window or curled up in a chair? Keep your mind open all the time, trying hard to see the place through objective eyes. What does your home tell you about the people who live there? Is it a happy home? Does it nourish your soul? If not, ask it why.

Right **In ancient Greece and Rome the hallway was considered a place between two worlds. Does your hallway offer somewhere for guests to pause and adjust to moving from one area to another?**

TALKING TO YOUR HOME

This may sound completely insane, but it does seeem to produce results. If you really want to put the soul back into your home, you should simply stand in the middle or the heart of your house and talk to it. Before you do you may like to run through the preliminary exercises on page 37 to relax yourself and open up your unconscious. Then stand or sit quietly at whichever spot you feel embodies the heart of your home. Allow yourself a few moments to center yourself quietly and breathe. It's best to do this in silence, when you're alone in the house. Now quietly and respectfully greet the house and ask if it's willing to talk to you. Houses are like people – some are easy to get to know and chatter quite happily to total strangers; others are more aloof, maybe shy, overly dignified or even downright rude. Remember you may have lived in your house for years and never bothered to talk to it before so don't be offended if it doesn't race to embrace your new relationship. What happens next varies from person to person. Some can 'hear' the house speaking in their heads. For some it feels like active imagination – they

imagine what the house might say. Others say they just get a feeling, or the odd word, or an image. Some people don't feel anything at all. So, if it doesn't work for you, you're not the only one in the world. Keep trying from time to time (and don't try too hard; it's one of those odd things that doesn't respond to willpower).

If you feel the house is responding you can ask it questions:
- Is it happy or unhappy?
- What would it like you to do for it?
- What could it do for you – and how?
- Is there anything specific it can suggest?

A technique from Gestalt psychology can be used to elicit answers. Place two chairs or cushions on the floor. One is 'your spot', the other represents the house. Sit on your spot and ask your question to the house's spot. Then shift places and answer as if you were the house. Shift back and forwards as you hold a conversation. Many houses simply feel neglected. They want to be looked after and loved. Some would adore a spring clean. Others may hate what you've done to them: Artexed ceilings that don't allow them to breathe; fake walls which cut up their space. Find out what your house wants. Ten to one, it will end up suiting your purposes as well.

WHO LIVES IN YOUR HOME?

If you live on your own, you can engineer your space precisely the way you want it. If, however, you share with other people, you are going to have to make compromises of some sort. We all have varying requirements, and a home needs to reflect everyone's wishes and desires. Now is the time for some practicality. Draw up a floor plan of your home. It doesn't need to be draughtsman quality but try to get the proportions roughly accurate.

If your home is on several floors do a plan for each. This will also come in useful for the feng shui work coming later, so make a few copies and keep one or two in reserve. Take one copy and label each room on your plan. Now put in the major pieces of furniture to mark out each room. Look at the plan and think about who uses which space. Pick a color for each person in the home and color in 'their' places. Someone might have a special chair which is supremely theirs. Someone might do all the cooking or it might be shared. Let the colors show the division of tasks. You might eat on a table but it could be commandeered by children for homework. Now, is it just the table or chair which 'belongs' to these people or does it feel as if their influence spreads throughout the whole room? Can anyone else use the room while they are there? Balance out how much each person uses each room and color in the room accordingly. What you end up with might be surprising. You may have colonized huge parts of the house or you might realize that you've been virtually squeezed out. The children may have no place to call their own. Certain rooms may be out of bounds to certain people. Have a good long think about why this might be so – and whether it serves your lifestyle.

If the other inhabitants of the house are up for it, give them their own plan of the house and get them to do the same exercise. You may find everyone agrees – or that you all have varying ideas about who 'owns' or shares what.

This part of the process is actually crucial to feeling at home in your place. We need to know and feel happy with our boundaries. Ideally, get everyone who shares the home to sit down and discuss what has come up in this exercise. Is the division of space fair? Who wants or needs more (children and teenagers will undoubtedly speak loudest here – but maybe adults as well)? Can you think of ways, together, that would give everyone what they need? Often this seems impossible but you can usually find a way. Maybe some people only need particular spaces at certain times. It could be fine for the kitchen to be a homework zone between certain hours, providing the books are cleared away afterward so you can use the table for your pottery or writing your novel. Children sharing a bedroom need to have their 'own' walls for posters and so on – or they could divide their space with furniture or a decorative screen. If your bedroom has been colonized as a study by your partner (and there is nowhere else the work paraphernalia could live) then again, a screen might be the answer to hide it away – and insist the phone is switched off and the answering machine switched on at night and weekends (and preferably shifted to another room during bedroom hours). Can't come up with any solutions at all? Ask your house.

By now you're probably yearning to make changes to your home. If they are small ones or involve shifting the use of various rooms to suit the inhabitants, then go right ahead. But don't make huge changes yet. A soul home is not something you can create overnight – it is an idea which grows and shifts, softens and mellows the more you think about it. So don't spend a fortune on calling in builders and decorators, or racing out and buying new furniture at this stage. Bide your time.

There are, however, a few simple adjustments you could make at this point. If you're itching to get going, try these...

FIRST MOVES

Make your threshold somewhere to pause. You might position a chair or settle there, with a stand for umbrellas perhaps. It's a good idea to take your outdoor shoes off before you walk into the house – to keep the house clean, not just physically but also psychically.

Make sure the first scent your nose (and those of your guests) encounters is pleasant. Place a bowl of fresh pot pourri in the hallway or polish any wood with lavender oil-scented furniture or floor polish.

Think about the various gods, spirits and angels of the house as you walk through your space. Who lives where? You may like to make each room sacred by having a representation of its guardian there: a little statue of Mercury in your study; flowers for Aphrodite in the bedroom; a candle for Hestia in your kitchen plus a decoration of corn (a decorative sheaf in the fireplace in summer or a corn dolly) for Demeter.

Shared rooms should be welcoming. Is your living room a place where everyone can feel relaxed? Or is it the kind of place where you are perpetually worried about marks on the furniture, sticky

Communal rooms, such as kitchens, should be places where the whole family congregates to eat and socialize. Furniture in these rooms should be people-friendly. With a scrub-top table, no one worries about spillages.

fingers on tables, stains on the carpet? Some people keep their 'best' room for entertaining, but can guests truly feel comfortable and 'at home' if they have to worry about dropping or spilling anything? If you're wedded to minimalism – white carpets and pure silk covers – why not keep them in your private space where, if anything happens to them, there's no one else to blame? Family and public areas should really be easy-going places – with strong, washable fabrics; easily cleaned rugs over tough wood or tile flooring. Precious ornaments could be kept safely in a locked glass cabinet to prevent children, animals or clumsy adults having hideous disasters. A scrub-top table in the

kitchen or breakfast room is the ultimate people-friendly piece of furniture. Spill food or wine on it and simply scrub it off. If a young artist's crayon slips or her paintbrush misses the paper, scrub it off. Everyone relaxes.

Ask yourself what mood you want in each room. Some rooms should be quiet, calm and relaxing while others might need to be energizing and dynamic. You might want to collapse into a semi-comatose state in your sitting room but need to keep alert and creative in your work room or study. See if your rooms are answering your needs – and the needs of the other people who share them. Would it be better to shift things around so the energy of each room matches all the activities which take place in it? For example, might your home office be better hidden in the dining room (with its lively atmosphere) than in your bedroom where you need to retreat and relax?

PART 3

the clear, clean home

decluttering

It is easy to guess one of the things you noticed as you toured your home. Clutter. Stuff. Junk. Piles of books, magazines and papers. Closets and chests jam-packed with clothes. Drawers full of bits – keys from forgotten locks; buttons from long-gone jackets; old receipts and notes; a dusty throat lozenge; a button; a few elastic bands. Don't feel guilty: we've all got it. Everyone has junk, apart from those unreal, robot-like people who live in glossy home-magazine minimalism – they probably have got stuff too (they just have bigger closets!)

You may be attached to your clutter or you may loathe it but, whatever your attitude, you need to clear it. You've heard this before; you've read it in a host of magazine articles and in every book on feng shui. So why this war on mess? Surely we don't want our homes to become impersonal, empty wildernesses? Well of course not. But there is a world of difference between a home which reflects its owner's personality in carefully chosen objects, magazines and books and one which is so jam-packed with stuff that your mind reels.

First and foremost, it is very hard to feel relaxed and comfortable in a home which is messy. On a physical level, clutter attracts dust which makes many people sneeze or have other allergic reactions. On a psychological level, clutter irritates the mind; it reminds us of things which need doing, fixing, finishing, starting even.

If you have a pile of papers in your room your energy automatically dips because you know it needs attention…every time you walk into your home and there are things that need repairing, letters that need answering, junk that needs clearing, your energy can't flow internally because of what is happening externally.

Karen Kingston, Space Clearer

One of the major benefits of good design is that there is a place for everything – here, bottles take their place in an integral rack and trays and other large items can be slotted into the side of the work surface.

CLUTTER – BLOCKING THE HOME'S LIFE BLOOD

Mess and clutter don't just affect us, however, they also affect the homes we live in. In the dictionary you discover that clutter means confusion, a confused heap, turmoil, din. It is also a variant of 'clotter' which means to run into clots. Imagine your home as a body. In our bodies, blood runs through our arteries, veins and capillaries. If, for any reason (smoking, bad diet, too little exercise etc.), these blood vessels become furred and thick-walled, the blood cannot pump effectively through the body. If the blockage becomes too extreme, the blood cannot squeeze through. Sluggish blood flow is one of the major causes of blood clots which, in turn, can lead to heart attacks or strokes. In a house the equivalent to life blood is energy, or chi. If the energy in your house cannot circulate easily, it

becomes stagnant and sluggish, Just like the blood. Nothing affects this subtle energy as much as piles of rubbish or unfinished business. So imagine that all those piles of papers and books, the broken tennis rackets and fishing nets, the drawers stuffed with old clothes are clogging up the arteries of your house. The solution suddenly becomes really obvious: clear them out.

Glass jars are great for storing herbs, spices and other dry goods. They look good and the contents are clearly visible.

THE BIG CLEAR-OUT

The first major practical step you can make to rejuvenate and restore your home is to clear the mess. It's not a particularly 'soulful' exercise you might think, but it is essential. There is no 'correct' way of doing it. Lots of books recommend you take it easy – do a drawer at a time or spend an hour a week. You may not have the patience for that if you are a 'plunge in and get it over with' type. You may be the sort of person who every so often has either minor or major purges. Something will set you off: you'll trip over something or have no room to put a book on a shelf, or not be able to find a receipt.

Some people's decluttering tends to be fast and furious – and very brutal. But that may not be for you. If this is new (or difficult) for you, take it easy. The great thing about decluttering is that you can always do more.

Take another trip around your home, this time on the lookout for mess and clutter. Identify all the problem areas. Some will stand out like sore thumbs. But it's not a case of 'out of sight, out of mind'; you need to go beyond cosmetic anti-clutter and check all those hidden places too: behind the sofa; in your closets and cupboards; drawers and dressers; attics, cellars and sheds. It may not be noticeable on a physical level but psychologically it's still clutter and, however subconsciously, you know it's there and it's affecting you.

Decide which area you will tackle first and get prepared. Wear old clothes and bring out a series of cardboard boxes or large rubbish bags to sort things into. Some stuff is pure garbage and the only place for it is the trash. Other things might be useful to someone else, so put them into one box or bag. Yet more may belong to other people. Sort out everything and then dispose of it in whichever way you choose. It helps to think that your old junk will give someone else pleasure so you could consider giving all your clutter to charity shops.

When the junk belongs to your family, why not give them a certain amount of time (a couple of hours? a weekend?) to claim any belongings they really want. After that, out they go. Kindergardens and nursery schools might be grateful for any old toys and games. Clothes might be welcomed at a women's refuge or a center for the homeless, or sold off to work colleagues to help fund your next shopping trip.

Still finding this hard? Let's go through the various kinds of clutter you are likely to encounter...

Right **An expansive, wide-mouthed wastepaper basket will prove a valuable piece of equipment when you begin to declutter you home in earnest. When dealing with junk mail, the best thing to do is to open your post standing or sitting directly over it, so every unwanted page hits the target.**

CLOTHES

It's tough getting rid of clothes as they tend to have a lot of sentimental value. 'It might come back into fashion'; 'I'll be able to wear it when I lose weight' are two common excuses, and it's not just women who hoard clothes either. A certain amount of sentimentality is fine. Keep the dress or shirt you wore for that first date of course; just don't keep every dress and every shirt you wore for every date. Ask yourself these questions:

- Have you worn it in the last two years?
- Is it out of fashion?
- Is it too big or too small?
- Is it stained or ripped?
- Was it an expensive impulse buy you now regret?

Any of these are good reasons to get it out of your life. It won't come back into fashion – at least not in the same way. There will always be something slightly different: the hemline will be longer;

the sleeves wider; the print will be carnations instead of roses. You can't win with the fashion business – they don't make money from people hoarding clothes, and anything less than 20 years old will never be fashionable (at least not for another 20 years and are you really prepared to wait that long?)

OK, so you're going to diet and get into those old clothes. Great, but why not treat yourself to some new ones when you reach your ideal weight? Use it as an incentive. Clothes that don't fit will always make you feel guilty, and guilt is the very worst way to make yourself lose weight. It doesn't work. So get rid of them, accept where you are at the moment, and as those clothes become too loose, treat yourself to more.

MAGAZINES AND NEWSPAPERS

You've already found out what to do with all those old magazines – use them for your journal and treasure maps. And once you've carved and snipped your way through a magazine, it loses its pristine beauty and is much easier to dump. Take them to a recycling center if they're really trashed, or maybe a friend who is also reading this book could make use of them. If you tell yourself you keep magazines for the recipes, go through and cut out the ones you want (be honest now, which will you really use?) and paste them in a cook's notebook. Do the same with gardening tips. You have to realize one essential thing about most magazines: they repeat the same features every year so you won't really be missing anything. If you don't believe this, check a few: gardens are seasonal creatures and the same tips (planting bulbs, dividing perennials, choosing roses etc.) crop up every year at around the same time. House magazines will always run another feature on choosing a kitchen; doing up a bathroom; planning a conservatory (because they attract advertisers that way) so you won't miss out if you throw away a whole back catalogue. Women's magazines are no different. They regularly run the same features again and again: how to revamp your sex life; how to give your relationship a MOT and so on.

The only things that change are news and fashion. If you're a teenager you might need to keep abreast of the latest trend. If you're a grown-up you can catch up on the latest fashions at the hairdressers (much cheaper than buying all the magazines). But if

Right **Some people are born collectors; their homes are full to the gills with pieces of furniture and belongings that are not in regular use. If you fall into this category, you may find the decluttering process painful.**

you do buy them they will be out of date within three months – so bin them.

Newspapers need regular pruning too. Nowadays, with good public libraries and the Internet, there's no excuse for hoarding papers for reference. Take cuttings, if you feel the need, and file them neatly. Then recycle the papers once a week.

PAPERS

You can't escape bits of paper. Bills, receipts, notes, letters and circulars breed like rabbits. But you can control them. Always tick the box asking that your details do not go on mailing lists when you send off for products by mail order or enter competitions. Put junk mail straight in the bin – or send it straight back saying you don't want it and asking to be taken off their list. One useful tip taught at time-management courses is to open your post standing or sitting by your wastepaper bin.

Clothes can be among the most difficult things to get rid of, because they carry such a lot of sentimental value. Weed out all you can, then hide the rest behind a screen until the next session.

Unless it needs a reply or is really useful, put it straight in the bin. Now you should be left with the essential stuff. Here it helps to have a system. In an ideal world you will deal with every piece of paper as it arrives. But who lives in an ideal world? So buy some of those attractive storage boxes – or cover shoe boxes with fabric or paint. You could have one for bills, one for tax receipts, one for letters and so on. As they arrive put them in the relevant box. But don't forget to deal with them. Once they're dealt with, either get rid of them or file them if need be.

Every house should have its own 'essential papers' file, containing insurance policies, mortgage documents, investments, tax details, licences and guarantees, etc., all neatly filed away. Use box files or a filing cabinet for other essential reference material (but make sure it really is essential). Go through your files once a year and check it's still valid.

BOOKS

Books are wonderful things; they can furnish a home and they impart knowledge, creativity, imagination and escapism. But they do need to be kept in their place. It's worth investing in attractive bookshelves and making a feature out of your books. Check that you need them all. Reference books, classics, old favorites, sentimental tomes – fine. But old pot-boilers you'll never read again; holiday trash novels; out-of-date guides? Give them to the charity shop and make room for more.

KITCHEN CLUTTER

Kitchens are storehouses for clutter: gadgets you never use; unwanted presents (fondue sets, waffle makers, woks, etc.); burnt-out saucepans; non-stick frying pans which now stick; mugs you loathe? We've all got them. If they're broken, bin them. If you simply hate them, see if anyone you know would like them, or advertise in the local paper. Or donate to a good cause. Anything that's chipped or cracked or broken simply isn't hygienic – so in the bin with it.

MISCELLANEOUS

Old LPs? Put your favorites on tape and sell the vinyl to a specialist record shop. Photos? Spend an evening sorting out the ones you love and put them in albums or in a special box. The ones where you look grim; the fifth attempt at that sunset; the hazy back-of-head shot? In the bin. Odd earrings? You'll never find the other one so bin them or give them to a children's playgroup for dressing up. Old keys, odd fuses, screws, nails and so on. Get rid of them – unless you want to put them tidily in a tool box. Cosmetics? You shouldn't keep cosmetics for years – like medicines, they have a use-by date. If you've had any skincare products over a year, bin them. Ditto make-up you've had for more than two years. Medicines? Check their use-by dates and sling the old ones.

By now you should have acres of extra space. Your home should be feeling clearer, more open, more expansive – and so should your thoughts. However, there are still likely to be one or two problem areas…

Stuff that's too expensive to throw out. You don't want it but it cost so much you can't bear to think of getting rid of it. OK, try to sell it. Get some of your money back. Or give it to someone who would really love it but couldn't normally afford something like that. Enjoy the warm feeling you get from helping someone else – an added bonus.

Nostalgic, family things. These are really ghastly. The old heirloom you loathe and abhor but don't dare get rid of because the family would be horrified or you would feel guilty. Don't feel guilty; just accept that it isn't right for you. Is there someone else in the family who would like it? If no-one wants it, even when you threaten to chuck it, then is it really such a precious heirloom or are you just the mug who has been dumped with everyone's collective guilt? If so, sell it. Treat the family to a celebration dinner with the proceeds.

Unwanted gifts. Some people say you should be brutally honest and tell the person that it's not your taste but, frankly, that's rude. One way of dealing with this is to keep the gift and bring it out when the giver comes around. You can then manufacture a series of 'accidents' when sadly things do get broken and need to be thrown out.

If you get really stuck at any point, stop and think how wonderful your house would look without the clutter. Close your eyes and imagine a home that feels free and easy and welcoming. The Chinese sages say that when you throw out clutter you are making room for something new and exciting to come into your life. Hold onto that thought as you bravely clear out the old to make way for the new.

spring cleaning

few of us actively enjoy cleaning. It's hard work, it's far from glamorous and, to be honest, there are plenty of things we'd rather do with our time. In fact, when you talk to people nowadays, it becomes obvious that there is far less cleaning going on than ever before. Many of us will remember hearing the sound of the vacuum cleaner every day of our childhood. As we walked to school women would be cleaning the front step and shaking out mats and dusters. Of course, these days we don't have time or we would rather spend what free time we do have in

other, more entertaining, ways. So, if we can afford it, we hire someone to clean our space or, if we don't, we fit it in where we can. We race round if guests are coming or wipe a cursory cloth over the worst grime. And so cleaning becomes an activity we begrudge. The suggestion is not that we've got it all wrong and that women should get back where they belong – on their hands and knees scrubbing. For a start, cleaning is an occupation for both men and women. But there is a real need, both physical and spiritual, for clean homes – and fortunately there are ways of salvaging the cleaning process so it becomes far less of a chore.

There is a reason why this cleaning process is so useful; why we all, men and women alike, should do our regular share of housework. Not just waving a duster in the air but rolling up our sleeves and putting in some elbow grease; scrubbing floors, clearing drains,

Left **Although most of us would say we actively dislike cleaning, it can provide the perfect balance to the cerebral, sedentary work many of us do to earn a living. And there's no doubt, modern fixtures and fittings make the job easier for us than it was for previous generations.**

scouring lavatory bowls. Not necessarily every day, but regularly. This activity is important because it's the perfect balance to the work so many of us do nowadays. More and more of us earn our livelihood via our heads. We sit slumped all day in chairs, staring at computer screens or battling with machinery. Cleaning, which when done properly is hard physical graft, provides a good healthy balance.

Left **A well-scrubbed bath-room with gleaming taps and a sparkling sink is a pleasure to behold and use; creating it will do your soul good too!**

– all need to be balanced. And yet we always strive for the light, for the bright, for success, for the sun. However, we cannot live in the light without acknowledging the dark. This may all sound very metaphysical and a long way from the kitchen floor, but there is a practical connection. For by physically cleaning, by getting down to the earth on our hands and knees, by clearing our muck and mess and dirt, we can keep the shadow balanced. We are embracing the dark. We are putting ourselves back in our place. Robert Johnson, author of *Owning Your Own Shadow*, describes this process perfectly with the example of the famous Jungians Dr Marie-Louise von Franz and Barbara Hannah, who shared a house in Switzerland. He explains how they:

> *...had the custom of requiring whoever had some especially good fortune to carry out the garbage for the week. This is a simple but powerful act. Symbolically speaking, they were playing out the shadow side of something positive.*

So clean for your soul's sake. Especially if you have had a brilliant day at work and are feeling full of righteous self-satisfaction. Particularly if you have had praise and are feeling proud and maybe just a touch superior or supercilious. Then, and especially then, go for the grimiest jobs in the house so no-one else has to bear the brunt of your shadow asserting itself.

CLEANING – CLEARING THE SHADOW

There is also a profound psychological advantage. In Jungian terms, the slog of cleaning can be a powerful way of dealing with the 'shadow'; the 'dark' side of the psyche. All through our daily lives we wobble on a kind of seesaw: if we play out characteristics from our acceptable, social persona, then we also inevitably balance them by playing out characteristics from the hidden shadow. Good and evil, positive and negative, light and dark, yin and yang, muck and brass

> *Are there some deep losses we might all incur from not cleaning up after ourselves? There is some sacredness in this daily, thoughtful, and very grounding housework that we cannot afford to lose if we are to be whole, integrated...For in this gesture of bended knees is some humility, some meditation, some time to recognize the first foundation of our homes.*
>
> Brenda Peterson, author of *Nature and Other Mothers*

Grounding is the operative word. When we clean, we connect with the ground, we take ourselves literally down to its level. The same process happens when we are gardening, when we plunge our hands into the soil of the earth. We are getting in touch with our base, our origin, our ultimate home. We are saved from the flights of fancy of the ego; we are put back in touch with the base chakra, the grounding earth beneath out feet.

HOUSEWORK FOR THE SOUL

In many cultures, cleaning is not only essential work for the soul, but is even considered to be a form of worship in itself. The Shakers considered work to be good for the soul and a way of glorifying God. 'Put your hands to work and your hearts to God,' said Shaker Ann Lee in a calling cry to the joys of housework. Each task was performed to the highest possible standard, with pride and a sense of joy. It's an inspiring idea. So, too, is space-clearing expert Karen Kingston's lovely description of her adopted land of Bali:

> *Soon after dawn in Bali, the swishing sound of rhythmic, methodical sweeping fills the air. It is somehow restful, comforting, does not disturb your sleep but rather adds a new dimension to it. They are using stiff brushes made from coconut leaf spines. This is happening everywhere on the island. Every piece of land near human habitation and every home, building and temple, is swept clean at the start of each day, and at intervals throughout the day as required. Purification is such an intrinsic part of this remarkable culture that it is no surprise that this fundamental practice is so deeply ingrained into the way of life.*

Karen Kingston, Space Clearer (from *Creating Sacred Space with Feng Shui*)

Several lessons can be learned from this description. Firstly, the Balinese perform their cleaning as a habitual practice, as we might brush our teeth or switch on the television. Anything which becomes a habit is more easily done. Secondly, they perform their cleaning in an unhurried, 'rhythmic' way. They take their time; the act has meaning for them and is an important ritual, so they do not feel it is time wasted and they do not resent doing it. And thirdly, they know it brings about purification – not just physical purification, but spiritual too. They are cleaning their homes, workplaces and temples in exactly the same way: all are purified, cleansed, made holy. What a beautiful idea. It serves to redeem that strange and rather po-faced saying 'cleanliness is next to godliness'.

If we can carry these ideas into our own cleansing rituals, housework becomes soul work. It stops being such a drudge when we realize we are sweeping out old thoughts, rigid ideas, and moribund emotions along with the dust; that by cleansing the physical environment we live in, we are also symbolically purifying our homes of negative and outworn attitudes and feelings that have been with us for too long.

By giving meaning to an everyday task, we bestow it with a sense of the sacred. It becomes a ritual rather than a chore. Some people say they can use the time they spend cleaning as a form of meditation, but most of us are not that enlightened. However, it is possible to see how focusing on the task and imagining that you are chasing away all the negative to make way for new, fresh, hopeful things can be inspiring. There is also something wonderfully satisfying about a space that has been cleaned – and cleaned thoroughly so that every surface sparkles; it's like starting from scratch, with a clean slate; making a new beginning.

Right **Try to keep bathrooms relatively clear and free of clutter to aid the cleaning ritual – it helps if it is not necessary for the person doing the cleaning to move piles of towels, bottles and knick-knacks before the hard graft can begin.**

CLEANING WITHOUT TEARS

Think about the following ideas – they all make the cleaning process more palatable – and even pleasurable:

Accept that cleaning is as ephemeral as the wind. You can't turn back dust. But don't use that as an excuse not to bother. After all, flowers don't last forever but that doesn't prevent us bringing them into the house and enjoying their beauty. Try to find a regular time for cleaning – maybe even 10 minutes a day. Use it as quiet, Hestia time. Focus on one task at a time. Become absorbed in what you are doing. Imagine you are as focused as a Shaker, or a Balinese sweeper. Be serene when you clean. If that's not possible, remember that the poet Stevie Smith apparently composed her best poems while vacuuming.

Choose your cleaning tools with care. Karen Kingston describes the Balinese brushes made from coconut leaf spines which sounds very romantic. But we have our own good tools of housework, available from any traditional hardware store. Pick a solid wooden-handled broom, one that feels comfortable to the grip. Choose sturdy bristle brushes, again with wooden backs. Track down an enamel or tin bucket, and use natural cotton cloths. On the other hand, you might be entranced by the vivid colors of modern plastics. It doesn't matter really – choose whatever speaks to your soul and your sense of fun. Plastic gloves with huge flowers around the wrist? Why not?

If the idea of quiet, contemplative time doesn't appeal, then maybe put on your favorite music – some poeple find they will clean far more vigorously to a raunchy rock track; others might prefer Vivaldi. Vacuum to the rhythm, scrub in time. And remember that heavy-duty housework can burn as many calories as a workout – so put some elbow grease into it.

Modern cleaning materials are mostly synthetic and pretty unpleasant. They do damage to the environment and can cause allergic reactions. They also smell fake. So try to use environmentally-friendly products if you can. Or make your own. There are several books which give lovely recipes for your own household products: seek out *Clean House, Clean Planet*; *Natural Housekeeping*; plus sections of *The Fragrant Pharmacy* and *The Bloomsbury Encyclopedia of Aromatherapy* (details of these and other helpful books can be found in the Bibliography on page 182).

Left **Sweeping stone floors can feel like a pointless chore as the dust soon reappears. But try to accept this without using it as an excuse not to bother.**

natural cleaning products

- Using essential oils in cleaning makes the house smell wonderful and perks you up as you clean as well. Try adding around 10 drops of your favorite essential oil to a cotton ball and then putting it in the bag of your vacuum cleaner. Change the oil to suit your mood. Wash down paintwork with water to which you've added a few drops of essential oil – or put a couple of drops on your cloth. Use grapefruit on a scrub-top kitchen table. You could try other fruity oils such as lemon and lime, or geranium and lavender for a bright summer scent, and warmer oils for winter, such as orange or mandarin, cypress, cedarwood and rosewood.

- Chrissie Wildwood, an aromatherapist who puts her oils to work around the house, suggests making your own furniture polish. Here's how: grate 30g (1oz) of yellow beeswax (from antique furniture dealers, craft shops or herbal suppliers), then heat with 125ml (4fl oz) of linseed oil (from hardware shops) in a heat-proof basin over a pan of simmering water. Stir well, then remove from the heat. As soon as the mixture begins to thicken, stir in eight drops of cedarwood essential oil and six drops of either rosemary or sandalwood. Spoon the mixture into a glass pot and use as you would a normal wax polish – apply with one duster and buff with another. The scent is wonderful – a subtle yet exotic aroma.

- Another idea from Chrissie Wildwood is to make your own carpet freshener. Take 225g (8oz) of bicarbonate of soda and 35–45 drops of essential oil. Put the bicarb in a polythene bag and then sprinkle with the oil and mix well. Seal the bag tightly and allow the aroma to permeate for at least 24 hours. Sprinkle over the carpet, leave for at least half an hour and then vacuum as normal. The oils you choose are up to you. A particularly pleasant combination is Chrissie's recipe called 'Persian Dream' which uses 25 drops of cedarwood, 10 drops of coriander and 10 drops of lemon – fresh and spicy.

the healthy home

by now you should have a clear, clean house. You are well on the way to making your home a healing haven, a true sanctuary. This part of the book contains a lot of very practical information which may seem a little dull, but it is all absolutely essential. However hard you try you will never get the most out of an environment which is not intrinsically clean, clear and healthy. All the space cleansing and feng shui in the world won't help a home which is dirty, unhygienic or full of potentially harmful chemicals and gases.

Many of us would prefer to shut our eyes and ears and hope that the thorny subject of pollution would just go away. It won't, unless we take action. By actively choosing healthy alternatives for your home and supporting companies which produce non-toxic and natural materials, you can help to change not only your own home, but also the world. A large claim but perfectly true. Any market can only survive if the demand is present for its products. If more of us demand safe, non-toxic, non-polluting furnishing, decorating, building and cleaning materials, more companies will be persuaded to produce them. There will be more choice, prices will fall and it will become far easier to protect your health and the wellbeing of the planet without sacrificing style or your pocket. You can create that market, that demand, and feel good in yourself that you are helping to protect the world. However, that's the wider issue. First and foremost, think about your home decoration for your own sake.

HAZARDS IN THE HOME

Our homes are, sadly, full of hidden hazards. Walk through your house and they are swarming all around you. Are your carpets synthetic or foam-backed? They are probably oozing volatile organic compounds (VOCs) such as formaldehyde. Do you have special stain-resistant finishes on your soft furnishings? They most likely leak organo-chlorines and phenols. There are VOCs and organo-chlorines all around the house: in building boards, bedding, paint solvents, adhesives, wood preservatives, household cleaners, air fresheners, polishes, and most plastic products. If your home lacks

adequate ventilation or you rarely open the windows, you may have high levels of pollutants building up unchecked in your home.

Domestic water is often polluted with chemicals such as chlorine and nitrates, not to mention bacteria. Radon gas can be transported through the water system and up into your tap and your drinking glass from many miles away. It has been estimated that there are around 70,000 synthetic chemicals in use worldwide, with another 1,000 added every year. The vast majority are unknown factors: they simply have not been tested fully. We don't know what they do to us, yet we trustingly take them into our homes.

As if all that were not enough, we are often suffering the ill effects of electro-stress in our modern homes. Electro-magnetic fields (EMFs) are all around us, created by all the gadgets and wonders of the modern world. From outside we are bombarded by radio waves, power lines, radar and satellite transmissions. From inside our homes we are embraced in the emissions from our televisions, faxes, photocopiers, computers, microwaves, mobile phones, night storage heaters, even from our bedside clocks. It has been estimated that our bodies are now handling up to 200 million times more electro-magnetic signals than those of our ancestors.

The effects on our health and wellbeing can be enormous. If we are healthy and have strong immune systems we can take a certain amount of bombardment, for a certain amount of time. But if we have weakened immune systems or suffer high levels of electro-stress and chemical pollution over a prolonged period of time, there are well-documented health risks. Electro-stress can cause tired-

Above **Wherever possible, use cleaning products made from natural, non-toxic materials. Try to make the most of natural daylight as you go about your daily tasks.**

ness and depression, headaches and a host of chronic diseases. Researchers blame ME, foetal abnormality and even cancer on electro-stress. Toxic chemicals have insidious effects too: many people are allergic to them and suffer asthma, eczema, migraine and chronic fatigue. Nausea, dizziness, heart irregularity, respiratory and eye problems, unexplained joint and muscle pain may all be blamed on chemical toxicity. And so too could problems of impaired judgment, irritability, mood swings and co-ordination difficulties. Not a cheery thought.

What can we do? First of all it helps just to be aware of the problems. Forewarned is forearmed. Baubiologie or Building Biology is a philosophy which began around 20 years ago in Germany and at last seems to have found its time. Its manifesto for healthy homes is as follows: fresh air; clean water; natural materials; generous daylight; suitable temperatures and humidity; protection from EMFs and avoidance of harmful earth energy (geopathic stress). The strategy is to identify the hazards in your home and take whatever steps you can to minimize or eliminate them.

TOWARDS A HEALTHY HOME

Few of us can afford to redecorate and refurnish our homes right away. But every time you need to redecorate a room or buy new furniture make sure you choose safe, non-toxic materials. Keep away from synthetic, foam-backed carpets: choose recycled wooden floors; natural floor coverings such as sisal, coir, seagrass, jute; 100 per cent wool or cotton/wool mix carpets and rugs. Natural linoleum comes in a vast range of subtle and vibrant shades and is easy to clean and very hygienic, so think about it, particularly if you have young children crawling on the floor.

Look out for paints which are water-based, milk-based, plant-based and mineral-based. If you want vibrant colors, use powdered pigments which you simply mix yourself. Pick natural thinners such as linseed oil and pine resin turpentine, and choose natural varnishes which allow the wood to breathe (they combine resins with scented turpentine and pigments). The added benefit is that they smell lovely.

Be careful when buying new furniture. Check what materials are used in the stuffing, base and fabric of sofas and chairs. Be very wary of treated materials – they may save stains but could be nasty to your health (maybe think about loose covers which can easily be washed instead). Recycled wood is a great option for tables, chairs, beds and cabinets. Many companies now use all old wood for their furniture which is not only safer for you but looks great too.

Pick 100 per cent natural fibers for your curtains, covers and bed linen. Organic unbleached cotton makes the most wonderful

When buying a new home check what materials have been used in the fittings – if you have the choice always opt for recycled wood rather than new.

sheets and duvet covers as it gets softer and softer the more you wash it. Snuggling up in them in the winter is pure heaven (but make sure your duvet is all natural too). In the summer, cool linen sheets are about the most inviting fabric you could put on your bed. Be particularly sure your children are sleeping in all pure materials. Many childhood allergies could be avoided this way. You may put off treating yourself to new bed linen but you should consider changing your children's sheets right away.

Turn off all electrical appliances and pull out the plug when they are not in use. Choose your television viewing with care, and sit as far away from the screen as possible. Don't ever fall asleep in front of the television and avoid having one in your bedroom. Be particularly careful with children who often tend to fall asleep watching television or have it on for excessive amounts of time.

Get rid of fluorescent lights and, where possible, replace all lightbulbs with full-spectrum light. If that's too expensive, make sure you use full-spectrum lighting at least for your work light or reading light. Lack of natural light can cause tiredness and depression. Maximize natural daylight by keeping curtains well pulled back, and blinds fully folded. Or go Scandinavian and cut out curtains altogether. Not ready to bare all? Use the sheerest of sheer fabrics to protect your privacy but let the light flood through. Try café curtains – covering the bottom half of the window only.

Trade in your electric blanket for a hot water bottle. Use a wind-up clock or a battery-operated alarm clock in your bedroom to avoid sleeping in an EMF from an electric clock. Make sure your bed is away from radiators and night-storage heaters.

It's hard to avoid the EMFs from computers but keep your machine turned off when not in use and use radiation screens. Wear natural fibers when working on a VDU. Laptop computers are a safer bet as they use liquid crystal displays which emit far lower EMFs, but don't work with it actually on your lap.

Use microwaves as little as possible – or not at all. The same with mobile phones. Be particularly wary in the home office – only switch on your photocopier when you actually need to use it.

Stock up on healing plants. Research from NASA showed that certain plants can remove up to 80 per cent of formaldehyde within 24 hours and that they can also absorb ozone, fumes from chemical cleaners, radon and cigarette smoke. Choose from these wonder plants: peace lilies; dwarf banana plants; golden pothos; peperomias; spider plants; mother-in-law's tongue (*Sansevieria*); Chinese evergreens (*Aglaonema*) and goosefoot plants (*Syngonium podophyl-*

lum). Keep at least one by your computer and television. The Cereus peruvianus ('*Monstrosus*') cactus, if you can track one down, is probably the very best to have by your computer as it can help to neutralize the harmful effects of VDUs. If you have a new carpet or have just painted a room, put as many of these plants in as possible and let them feast on all those nasty chemicals.

Install a water filter (reverse osmosis is good) under your sink – or at least buy a water filter jug for the fridge and put all your drinking and cooking water through it. Make sure boilers and furnaces are serviced regularly to reduce carbon monoxide leakage. Ensure ventilation is adequate.

Iron and steel in bed frames and sprung mattresses can become magnetic and leak EMFs. Test your bed by running a good compass slowly over it – if the needle deflects from North, the springs or mattress are likely to be magnetic. Be on the safe side and make sure your next bed is wood; your mattress made of natural products without metal springs.

If you live in an area where radon gas is a problem, have your home checked. There are solutions which can remedy the problem.

the air we breathe

- While you're waiting to redecorate or buy new, there are still plenty of things you can do. First of all, keep your home as well aired and ventilated as possible. Open the windows and let the air in – for at least 15 minutes twice a day. This also helps prevent excess humidity and stops the air getting stale. Install window and ceiling fans throughout the house and use exhaust (extractor) fans in kitchens and bathrooms.
- If your home has undue humidity, install extractor fans. If you have the opposite problem and your air is too dry (usually a result of central heating), increase humidity with bowls of fresh water or use it as an excuse to install a decorative waterfall (great feng shui – more about that in Part Four).
- Always use natural cleaning products, or make your own from aromatherapy products – much more pleasant to inhale than chemical fumes.

geopathic stress

geopathic stress is believed to be caused by abnormal energy fields generated by deep underground streams, large mineral deposits or faults in the substrata of the earth. It has been blamed as a major contributing factor in everything from migraines to cancer, from nightmares to divorce. It sounds like the latest scare story but the evidence suggests that geopathic stress certainly does exist. In Germany it has been researched since the 1920s and is taken very seriously. Experiments have shown that bacteria grow abnormally when grown over

underground currents of water, while mice inoculated with disease will fall ill far more rapidly when kept over a subterranean vein of water. Now builders in Germany and Austria test sites before building and many will routinely give guarantees that new buildings do not have lines of 'bad' energy passing through them.

However, the methods for testing for geopathic stress are far from reliable. Most people use dowsing, but this method has been known to come up with wildly different diagnoses. The 'cures' are equally unpredictable and many consumer watchdog organizations believe they are simply expensive placebos. On the other hand, some people are quite convinced they help.

So what do you do if you suspect your house is suffering from geopathic stress? First, don't panic – you won't need to move house! Geopathic stress moves in quite focused lines – most likely you would just need to move your bed or favorite chair. Find a dowser or expert who has no interest in selling you anything – professional dowsing societies may be able to put you in touch with someone local and reputable.

DETECTING GEOPATHIC STRESS

How can you tell if you have geopathic stress in your home? Dowsers say that typical signs of GS are feeling permanently tired and below par. Everything is an effort. You are easily depressed and irritable. Illnesses, aches and pains will not respond to any treatment. Children become disruptive and badly behaved.

Because GS comes up in thin lines it can easily affect just one person in the house – a line can pass through one side of the bed or one armchair. So don't expect everyone to suffer the same symptoms – or even to have symptoms.

If you suspect you suffer from GS, try putting cork tiles under your bed or favorite chair for a few weeks and see whether you start to feel better. The cork seems to neutralize the rays for a limited period. If you do start to feel better, try moving your bed or chair.

Watch where your pets sleep. Cats adore GS and will often choose to sleep on a bad spot while dogs will avoid it at all costs. If the cat always makes a beeline for your favorite armchair, try moving it to the dog's favorite spot. The downside to this one is that cats will also often follow their owners, so use your common sense here.

Babies are apparently very sensitive to GS. If your baby constantly rolls over to one corner of the cot, he or she may be attempting to escape GS. Move the cot to another part of the room and see whether the baby stays put.

Geopathic stress expert Jane Thurnell-Read suggests trying the following if you feel you are affected by GS: switch on a hairdryer and run it all over you with the side of the dryer touching your body. 'It sounds crazy,' admits Thurnell-Read, 'but if you do it once a week it does seem to help.'

Experts suggest that geopathic stress moves in quite focussed, thin lines, so you may well find that one end of the sofa is badly affected, while the other end suffers no ill-effects at all.

the energetic home

space clearing

t hanks to your hard work, your home should now be sparkling clean and free from clutter – well, at least, less cluttered than it was before. Stand still for a moment now, quietly, in the center of your home or in a major room. What do you notice? Does the house feel different at all? Walk through your home once more, with your antennae up – can you feel anything unusual? A clean, clutter-free home usually feels quite noticeably different from one which is dirty and clogged with stuff. Undoubtedly it will look better and smell better but it should also feel better.

If it does, congratulate yourself: you are becoming more sensitive to the atmosphere, the subtle energy, of your home. If it doesn't, don't worry: you will find that the work in this part of the book should help make you more sensitive to the living energy of the home. It will also make the atmosphere feel even better.

Every home, however large or small, is far more than walls, roof, floor and furniture. These factors generally stay put but there is another element to the home which is permanently shifting, moving, changing. This is the subtle energy of the home. In China this energy is known as *chi* or *qi*. In India it is recognized as *prana*. The Japanese call it *ki*, and in the Middle East it is known as *qawa*. These ancient cultures have known for millennia what modern physics is only just discovering: that everything around us, whether it's a tree, a dog or the kitchen table, is made up of energy.

> *Your home is not just a composite of materials thrown together for shelter and comfort. Every cubic centimeter, whether solid or seemingly empty space, is filled with infinite vibrating energy fields.*
>
> Denise Linn, Space Clearer

While the science remains mind-bogglingly baffling for most of us, we can all understand the theory in practice. If you've had a terrible argument, the room seems heavy and tense. We use the

A clean, clutter-free home has its own special atmosphere of serenity, and a feeling about it that is quite different from one that is dirty and clogged with uncherished furniture and 'stuff'.

phrase 'you could cut the air with a knife'. The mood during a lively party is different again.

SPACE CLEARING – PSYCHIC SPRING-CLEANING

In cultures where this concept of vital energy is understood, people spend as much time on psychic clearing as they do with their physical clearing. Denise Linn worked for years learning techniques from the Huna tradition of Hawaii and from Native Americans. Karen Kingston takes most of her practices from Bali, where space clearing is as much a part of life as their daily sweeping.

Unfortunately, in our technological societies, space clearing comes low down on our list of priorities. In fact, it's safe to say that few Western homes will ever have been space cleared – unless they are extremely old. For we did once have a tradition of clearing, back in the old days when our minds and souls were more open to unseen energies. And there are still vestiges of old space-clearing practices, if you look hard enough. The incense wafted around the church is cleansing the atmosphere; the bottle of champagne crashed against a new ship is a form of consecrating ritual; and the bells which ring out on a Sunday morning or to greet a newly mar-

Even if your living space is newly built and physically 'clear', space clearing may still be worthwhile to clear away any negativity left behind by the builders.

ried couple were not intended just to call worshippers to prayer or celebrate a marriage but also to cleanse the parish and the parishioners with healing sound.

You may well feel, looking at your newly clear, clean home, that cleansing the space itself is a bit unnecessary. But think of it like this. Imagine you hadn't physically cleaned a room for 10 years. No dusting, no vacuuming, no window cleaning – nothing. Imagine what it would look and feel like. It's a pretty unpleasant thought, isn't it? Now think about one of the major rooms in your home. What has gone on in that room over the last 10 years? You may have had good times there but equally you might have had rows, sat sobbing your heart out, felt depressed, angry or hopeless. Other people might have brought their negative feelings into that room. And what about the people who lived there before you? How do you know what energy they left behind them? Now realize that you've covered only the last 10 years. If you are living in an old building you could have decades, even centuries, of hate, fear, loathing, malice, sadness, jealousy, resentment and so forth built up like layers of grime. Of course, you might be lucky and have happy, joyous feelings sticking to the walls. But, even so, it's better to start afresh and build up your own personal psychic atmosphere.

Karen Kingston says that when you live somewhere with 'dirty' old energy, the signs are clear. Things will be unsatisfactory in a number of different areas – through no fault of your own.

> *Your life doesn't seem to move. You want it to go a particular way but nothing seems to happen. You might feel low in vitality or find you have the same problems recurring over and over again. You might even get more colds or be more constipated than other people.*
>
> Karen Kingston, Space Clearer

Even if you have just moved into a brand-new home, space clearing is still well worthwhile. The building site will have its own energy and even the builders, electricians, plumbers and decorators will have left their personal emotions, moods and energy in your space.

SENSING ENERGY

Before you launch into space clearing, it can help to be able to sense subtle energy. It sounds difficult but in fact most people will find it comes quite easily – providing you relax, lay your scepticism to one side and give yourself enough time.

First of all, wash your hands and take off any rings, bracelets, watches etc. Roll up your sleeves and sit down with your hands resting on your lap, slightly apart, palms facing upwards. Close your eyes.

- Relax your hands and begin to focus your attention on your palms and fingertips. If you feel tiny tingles of electricity on your skin, that is your own electro-magnetic energy.
- Now raise both hands to waist level and turn your palms to face each other – curve your palms as if they were holding a very soft imaginary ball about the size of a football.
- Bounce your palms towards each other as if you are gently squeezing and releasing the ball – you should feel energy flowing between your two palms. Now imagine the ball is bigger – beach ball size. Bring your palms together – to tennis ball width.
- Next you're going to use an NLP (neuro-linguistic programming) technique called anchoring to remember this body state. Be totally aware of precisely how you feel in this state and then swiftly clench one or both fists.
- Repeat the whole exercise again, and once again anchor the feeling with the clenched fist.
- Come out of the state – get up, walk around, shake your arms. Now try clenching your fist again and see if you can get back into the 'aware' state without all the preparation. If so, you've anchored – if not, you will need to go through the procedure a few more times, always ending with the clenched fist.
- Soon, whenever you clench your fist, you will find yourself in 'receptive' mode.

Once you have your energy sensors on tap you can start to feel energy in the home. First practise on plants and animals, even people. Try stroking a cat about six inches away from its fur – feel its energy – it may even respond as if you were physically stroking it. Try putting your hands over a living plant or bunch of flowers – the energy of healthy fresh plants is usually cool, like a pleasant breeze. Now experiment on objects – you may find that some give off a warm, gentle energy.

Get a friend to put out their hands with the palms facing you. Now put your hands up about six inches away from theirs – feel the energy.

If you practise these exercises carefully you will become more and more sensitive. Soon you will find you can distinguish between the energy of a healthy plant and one which is dying; some objects will feel good and comfortable; others will have a more unpleasant energy. This happens because objects pick up energy from the people and places around them. If you are a really adept sensitive, you can 'read' the whole history of an object just by holding it or feeling its energy.

PREPARING FOR SPACE CLEARING EXERCISES

Although space clearing is generally totally safe, there are several guidelines you should follow before clearing your home.

Don't perform space clearing if you feel scared or apprehensive. If you feel your house has any kind of evil or possession then you should seek out a trained professional (contact your local church or psychic center). Most of the energy in homes is just stuck or stale but some places do seem to have something heavier – call it a ghost, spirit, whatever – and you shouldn't try to shift that by yourself.

Choose a time for space clearing when you feel fit, healthy and emotionally balanced. It is also better for a woman not to perform space clearing while pregnant or menstruating as these are times when her energy should be turned inward rather than outward.

Before you space clear, ensure you have carried out all your decluttering and physical spring-cleaning. If not, go back to the sections on those subjects and get these basics covered first.

Spend time thinking about what you want to achieve with your space clearing. You should have a good clear idea by now (after Part

Right **You will soon become adept at sensing energy and may even be able to 'read' the whole history of an object just by placing your hands over its surface.**

Two) of what you wish for from your home. This is a good time to try to encapsulate those feelings into one or two sentences of clear intent, such as 'My home is a place of gentle serenity which embraces me with feelings of warmth, security and tenderness.' Or 'I want my home to be a clear, warm, supportive place.' How you put it is up to you but be clear in your mind about your intentions.

You need to be clean in your body as well as clear in your mind. So before you start work, have a shower or a bath (you could use a few drops of a purifying essential oil such as lavender, juniper or rosemary), wash your hair and brush your teeth. Put on clean, fresh, comfortable clothes. Keep off all jewelry and watches and avoid metal belts and buckles. If the weather is warm, it's best to be barefoot for space clearing. However, if you're space clearing in a cold house then wear cotton socks or leather-soled slippers.

Do not perform space clearing for anyone with mental or psychological problems. Call in an expert.

Now let's move on to the clearing itself.

CLEARING EXERCISES

Before you begin, take some time first of all to center yourself. Breathe deeply and evenly and allow yourself to feel calm and balanced. Visualize yourself surrounded by your aura, an egg-shaped cocoon filled with soft white light which is there to protect you and keep you safe from negative energy. Now expand that light to fill the whole of your home. If it feels more natural, you can choose another color: some people like to imagine pure blue light, a soft rosy pink, gold or golden pink.

Now you are prepared: Starting at the main entrance to your space, hold your hand a few inches away from the wall and start to 'sense' the energy. You should find, after the preliminary exercise, that this comes quite easily. Your palm should face the wall, with your hand roughly parallel with your shoulder and your arm fairly relaxed, not rigid. Move your hand along the wall in a motion similar to that of stroking a cat. You may find as you do this that you begin to get impressions, much as you did when you 'spoke' to your house in earlier chapters. Work around your home in this way, picking up feelings, sensing for 'dull' or 'stuck' spots where the energy feels sluggish or thick. These are the parts of your home that will need most attention later.

Now choose a way to get in touch with the spirit or spirits of your house. You may already be on good terms with them and know what they like. If not, the traditional ways to please the spirits are to light candles, burn incense, bring in fresh flowers and offer prayers. The method you choose is up to you and your beliefs. But put your whole intention into whatever you choose. Put an offering to the angels or spirits of your house in each room. An ideal offering is one which uses each of the four elements: these are most easily represented by a bunch of fresh flowers for earth, incense for air, the candle for fire and a bowl of pure water for water.

Left **Once you have centred yourself, and feel yourself surrounded by your protective aura, move to the main entrance of your living space and, with your palm facing the wall, start to sense the energy. Work around your home in this way, clapping each corner clear.**

The basic move of space clearing is clapping. Move steadily around your home systematically clapping into every corner, nook and cranny. It sounds so simple, but this is all it takes: you clap your hands into the corner, starting low and swiftly clapping on up toward the ceiling as high as you can. Repeat this as many times as necessary. You will know when you've clapped the corner clear because the sound of your clapping will become clearer. If you're still not sure, check the energy of the corner with your outstretched hand. As you clap, imagine your clapping is dispersing all the stagnant energy. That's it: now you just have to go around your whole space in the same way, sensing and dispersing the energy.

When you have finished your clapping, wash your hands thoroughly under running water to get rid of any negative energy you may have collected.

Most professional space clearers would now use a bell. If you have a bell with a really pure, clear tone, use that. Simply walk around your home again, this time ringing the bell as you go along. Your aim is to create a continuous circle of sound so you need to ring the bell again before the last tone has died away. When you get back to your starting point, draw a horizontal figure of eight in the air with your bell. If you don't have a suitable bell, don't worry – you will have already done some serious cleansing with your clapping alone.

Finally, you need to seal your newly energized and clean home. Fill the space once again with your expanded aura, imagining any remaining stagnant energy being pushed clean out of the house. Now you should shield the house. Stand at each corner of your home and imagine yourself bringing down a force-field of energy with a downward sweep of your arm. The four fields merge together and create a safe haven, protecting your work and cocooning your home.

FOLLOW YOUR INSTINCTS

It can take quite a time to build up expertise in space clearing. Remember that the experts often take years of training – Karen Kingston says that in Bali it can take a whole year just to learn how to ring a bell properly! But don't let that put you off. You will probably find that your intuition will take over once you try these techniques and you will discover that you know these rituals somewhere deep in your psyche. Even if you don't feel you've quite got the hang of it, rest assured that your efforts will be well rewarded.

So use these guidelines to space clearing as just that, guidelines. Follow your instincts, always keeping in touch with the feeling of the house, its guardians, your intuition and common sense. You shouldn't go far wrong.

smudging

One particular form of space clearing which is becoming very popular is smudging. Smudging has been a part of Native American ritual since time immemorial. Originally mixtures of sacred herbs and resins were burned in a special bowl: smoke was then wafted around the person or place needing purification and cleansing. However, smudge sticks (bundles of dried herbs tied together with colored thread or a strip of hide) offer an easier way of smudging which is just as effective. The herbs most often used in smudge sticks are sage and sweetgrass.

The Spirit of Sage has the power to drive out negative spirits and influences while sweetgrass is used to attract positive healing energy. Native Americans see smudge as a way of shifting between the various levels of reality – connecting us here in the material, physical world with the subtle realm of the spirit.

SELF-SMUDGING

This is a basic self-cleansing exercise which clears your aura and helps you feel balanced. It is an ideal exercise before any form of space clearing. You will need a smudge stick or loose, dried sage and/or sweetgrass, matches, a large feather and something in which to place your smoldering smudge (a small bowl, shell or saucer).

1. Light the end of your smudge stick and let it burn until the tip starts to smolder. Then extinguish the flame so the smudge stick smokes. Alternatively put your herbs into your bowl, light them, then blow out the flame so the herbs are smoldering.
2. Focus on the smoke as you quietly center yourself. Ask the spirits of the sacred herbs for help in your ceremony.
3. Waft the smoke towards your heart. Hold the smudge away from you and use the feather to waft the smoke toward you. Take the smoke over your head, along your arms and down the front of your body. Imagine the smoke lifting away the negative thoughts, emotions and energies that have attached themselves to you.
4. Now bring the smoke down the back of your body towards the ground. Visualize the last vestiges of negativity being taken back into the earth, away into the air.

5. Repeat, imagining the spirit of sweetgrass bringing healing, positive energy to you.

SPACE CLEARING

1. Light your smudge and smudge yourself.
2. Walk around the room wafting smoke into each corner. Call on the Spirit of Sage to drive away all negativity from the room. Then repeat, asking the Spirit of Sweetgrass to bring harmony and balance to the room.
3. Come to the center of the room and stand quietly for a few moments. Then send smudge to each corner of the room in turn asking the spirits of each direction to bring their particular energy to that space. Traditionally each direction is governed by a spirit animal. Buffalo governs the North, the element of Earth, which grounds and cleanses. Eagle rules the East, the element of Air which inspires. Coyote governs the South and Water which brings strength and peace. Grizzly Bear rules the West and Fire which brings energy and vitality. Imagine these great guardians bringing their energy to your space.
4. Now look upward, sending smudge up to the ceiling. Invoke the protection of Father Sky.
5. Finally squat towards the floor and send smudge down to the earth invoking the nurturing spirit of Mother Earth.
6. Put down your smudge stick and stand quietly with your eyes shut. Visualize all the great spirits you have summoned. Give thanks to all of them.

The sacred smoke of smudge was used by the native American Indians to cleanse and purify themselves and their surroundings. The smudging ritual calls on the four great animal spirits; Eagle in the east, Bear in the west, Buffalo in the north and Coyote in the south.

feng shui fundamentals

You probably already know a fair amount about feng shui. Over the last few years it has become increasingly popular in the West, with features in virtually every newspaper and a growing stack of self-help tomes on the bookstore shelves. At first the idea sounds crazy: how can shifting your furniture change your luck? How can repositioning a mirror bring in more money? Why on earth does it matter if there is a beam over your bed? It all sounds insane. However, if you've been following the preceding chapters in this book you should have

the building blocks to grasp how feng shui works. If you can believe that our homes are full of subtle energy, constantly moving, then it makes more sense that the layout of our homes, the positioning of our furniture and other features, can affect how that energy flows.

Feng shui evolved around 5,000 years ago in China. The ancient Chinese believed that invisible life energy (called *chi*) flowed through everything. It's the same philosophy that underlies

Left **Crystals and prisms are important feng shui cures. These appealing objects can be used to attract more chi to an area, or calm down or deflect chi that is moving too fast and racing out of a house as fast as it is coming in.**

acupuncture. If the energy in your body is flowing freely and easily, you will stay fit and healthy. If, however, the energy becomes stagnant or blocked, or erratic and undisciplined (through bad diet and lifestyle or weakness in an organ), you will most likely fall ill. The needles of acupuncture act simply by removing the blockages or calming the energy flow – they regulate the chi.

The principle is exactly the same in houses. The Chinese believed that the buildings we live in require just as much attention as our bodies and so developed this highly complex science for 'healing' the environment. Centuries of observation showed that different areas of the house and different parts of each room attracted specific energies. Furthermore, they discovered that certain configurations (the layout of rooms or even the position of furniture or features) could either help or hinder the free, smooth flowing of energy. If the energy was blocked or allowed to flow too swiftly it would cause corresponding blockages and problems in life. Clutter can 'catch' energy, stopping its free circulation and turning it dull and stagnant. Sharp corners can send energy shooting out in too harsh a concentration. A series of open doors sends energy racing through, too fast and too frenzied. A blank wall will stop the energy dead in its tracks.

Fortunately, however, the Chinese also realized that very small but specific changes (known as 'cures'), such as hanging wind chimes or crystals in certain places or using particular colors, would correct such disharmony and put your life back on track. Boosting some areas with auspicious colors and objects could even create better energy and opportunities in life. At its core, feng shui teaches that by making small shifts to your home you can affect everything in your life, from your finances to your health, from your relationships to your spirituality.

FROM HOLLYWOOD TO WALL STREET

Although feng shui sounds mystical, it is taken very seriously, not just in its native China but all over the world. Madonna is a fan; so is actor Pierce Brosnan. There have been rumors in the press that members of the British royal family have sought the help of feng shui experts. And, surprisingly, it is not necessarily Hollywood celebrities or troubled royals who are seeking the help of feng shui consultants. Most of their clients are high-powered businesspeople and large corporations who use feng shui to stay ahead of the game and to keep their profits high.

Western and Oriental banks, restaurants and corporations throughout Asia and also in the USA consult feng shui experts. Chase Manhattan, Citibank, Chase Asia, Paine Webber, Morgan Guaranty Trust, the American Chamber of Commerce and the offices of the *Asian Wall Street Journal* and the *Far Eastern Economic Review* (all sane, sage businesses) have used feng shui. Body Shop founder Anita Roddick freely stated that her headquarters and shops around the world had been designed using the principles. Richard Branson of the Virgin empire has used feng shui to huge advantage. And telecommunications company Orange have used it to rapidly expand their business.

People use feng shui because, quite simply, it works. A hotel in Australia was virtually empty until an Oriental company bought it and called in a feng shui consultant. He said the problem lay with

> *Today, those in powerful positions do not take chances where feng shui is concerned. I was surprised to find hard-nosed businessmen anxious to try feng shui as an added tool to clinch deals, enhance corporate clout, or expand their businesses.*
>
> Sarah Rossbach, Feng Shui expert

the staircase: it faced the front doors and so the hotel's energy was shooting outwards and being lost. The staircase was moved and the hotel's luck changed almost overnight. On a more personal level, feng shui consultant Sarah Shurety tells of a couple who were on the verge of divorce. They could hardly bear to talk to one another. Sarah checked their house and found the problem in their bedroom. There was a large beam in the ceiling above their bed which effectively divided their bed in half. In feng shui, beams are considered to cause quarrels and even ill-health in the people who sleep under them. Sarah advised the couple to move their bed. 'Now they are newly in love again,' she reports, 'the beam was cutting them in half, separating them.'

Above **Mirrors can cure a host of feng shui woes. In China, they use small octagonal mirrors, called ba-gua mirrors, to deflect away unpleasant energies.**

MAPPING YOUR HOME

Now it is time to see how feng shui could help your home. Having said that, feng shui is a complex science and this book does not attempt to explain every facet. If you have a house with an unusual layout or, particularly, an apartment which has been created out of an older building and so has a very odd shape, you may find it tricky to apply the rules to your own space. There are two options here: firstly you could employ a professional feng shui consultant. They don't come cheap but, if you find someone experienced and good, your investment should be well worthwhile.

The second option, however, is cheaper. Many modern feng shui consultants believe that much of feng shui's power relies on intuition and an awareness of subtle energy. Hopefully this will be a skill you are already developing. So, if the advice here doesn't take into account your curiously shaped abode, don't panic. Once again, center yourself, get in touch with the spirit of the house and see what comes into your mind. You may well find the answer within yourself.

To begin, there are some fundamental principles of feng shui we need to learn. The first is the ba-gua. This is an octagonal template which divides any space (your entire home or simply a room within it) into eight areas. These eight areas (or corners) represent wealth, fame, marriage, children, helpful people, career, knowledge and the family. Let's take a quick look at these areas and how they affect your life.

WEALTH

Wealth governs your finances, money and the material side of life. If you have problems with the wealth corner of your home – if it is missing, cluttered or blocked off – you will undoubtedly find money is tight. This area can also correspond to your feelings of abundance in general: you might feel 'rich' with blessings, full of *joie de vivre*, with a sense of happy wellbeing if this area is working well.

FAME

Yes, this area can apply to true fame but equally it shows how you are viewed by the outside world: your social standing, your place in the world. It also takes care of your self-esteem and confidence. If all is right with your fame corner, you will feel good about yourself and who you are.

MARRIAGE

Not just marriage, but all love relationships are governed by this corner. If you have unlucky relationships or would just like a relationship in the first place, this is one of the main areas on which you will need to concentrate. On a more esoteric level, this also represents your relationship with the wider world and, on a more intimate level, with yourself. We can't have good relationships with others unless we have a good relationship with ourselves.

CHILDREN

If you have children this is an area you will want to ensure runs smoothly. If you don't have children but would like them, this is an area to boost. If you don't have (or want) children and think this corner is one to avoid, think again. Another name for this corner is Creativity and it can boost your imagination and artistic endeavors or simply help you find creative answers to problems.

HELPFUL PEOPLE

Everyone can benefit from having helpful people in their life. Nurturing this corner makes sure the people you need greet you with a smiling face and a willingness to help. You could find help from unexpected places and people when this corner functions well – or simply that the plumber is swift, efficient and doesn't charge the earth.

CAREER

How do you earn your living? With ease or great difficulty? Are you happy in the work you do or would you love a change? This is the corner that needs to be kept smooth-running for ease in your employment; boosted if you want a higher profile; shifted if you want a change.

KNOWLEDGE

Knowledge covers a wide variety of ideas: this is the corner which can generate wisdom, ideas, learning and scholarship. If you, or anyone in the family, is studying, this corner will need attention. But equally it offers inner knowledge, spiritual wisdom, fresh ideas and inspiration.

THE FAMILY

Not only is our immediate family represented here, but our lineage, our ancestors too. This may sound a strange idea in the West but to the Chinese it is quite obvious. Keeping your ancestors happy results in good luck and prosperity. However, on a more practical level, this corner ensures that families get on together – not just the immediate family but your extended family, relatives and friends.

So you can see that, while you may have imagined that only one or two corners might need attention, if you want your life to run smoothly you really need to look at all the corners. This makes sense: a true home of the spirit is a balanced home. It should not just be a home which craves fame and money above knowledge and friendship. Nor can any home thrive on love and creativity alone: a certain amount of money and recognition will make life much more comfortable. So let's see how to plot the various corners in your house.

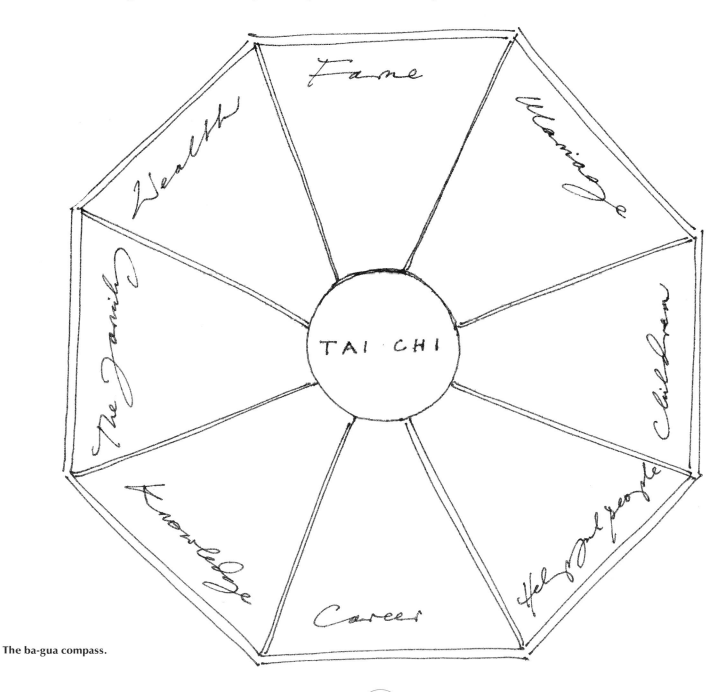

The ba-gua compass.

first steps to practical feng shui

the very simplest shifts can bring enormous, far-reaching effects in feng shui. So don't dismiss it – try it. What's to lose? You don't have to do everything suggested in these chapters all at once: just try one or two things to begin with and see what happens. Apart from anything else, feng shui often makes suggestions that are very practical, which make your home easier to run or more attractive. So be open-minded and give it a go. Once more, take a walk through your home. By now you're probably becoming very sensitive to its atmosphere and 'spirits'. You may

gently touch a wall as you pass, or caress the banister. You might whisper a soft 'hi' to the lares, smile gently at your guardian angel, or nod your head to Hestia as you pass the hearth. You could have a few friendly words with the home itself. Now take a few moments to get in touch with your own subtle energy, using the exercise on page 84. Feel the energy running through your hands, between your palms, like a magnetic charge. Now imagine the energy, the chi, running around your body: is it running smoothly and harmoniously, or racing through some places and becoming sluggish in others? If you have any health problems, this can be quite an illuminating and useful exercise in itself: you can often become very sensitive to how the chi is flowing within yourself and can then visualize it flowing in a more disciplined and healthy manner. But back to the house.

BECOMING THE CHI

Now you have got in touch with the chi, shift your perspective so you start to imagine you are the chi energy in your home. You want to flow through this space, to move freely and easily around the home. So you come through the front door and into the home. What greets you? Can you move smoothly through a well-planned space which is clear and clean? Or are there masses of sharp corners to spin off and badly positioned furniture to bump into? Would you get stuck in a morass of mess and clutter? Might you find yourself flying through far too fast because there are long corridors or a flight of stairs shooting straight up opposite the front

door? Could you come to a grinding halt because there's a wall right in front of you? Go around your home imagining you are the energy passing through the space and see what your intuition tells you. Is your home chi-friendly?

Now you have a feeling for feng shui on an intuitive level, let's take the ba-gua further. You've looked at the drawing of your home on a piece of paper with the ba-gua superimposed over it. Now you need to check your home equipped with your new feng shui knowledge.

MAPPING YOUR HOME WITH THE BA-GUA

Walk through your home with the ba-gua diagram in your hand. Make sure that the position of each room really is as you drew it on your map. Be on the lookout for more subtle features: you might think your space is perfectly square but once you look further you might see that there is a bit jutting out from one room; a bay window or a deep recess in another. These are important features so add them to your plan.

Now you can check to see whether each space is working at its best. For example, you may have a perfectly formed wealth area but be using it as a storeroom for junk. You might be sleeping in the children area while they are sleeping in the marriage corner (which would be perfect for your bedroom). Are you desperately trying to make it as a singer or keen to get publicity for your favorite charity and getting nowhere? Check the fame area – it might be hidden behind a pile of old clothes crammed in a closet; it might be in a bathroom which, to be honest, is less than pristine; it could be missing altogether. Don't worry for now if areas are missing: we'll look at how to cure that later.

There may be obvious changes you could make which involve no expense – just a little effort. If it's possible, try to site your bedroom in the marriage area. Children should obviously sleep in the children area, if at all possible. A living room would be wonderful in the family area; a study in the knowledge area. Helpful people or family is good for kitchens and breakfast rooms. You get the idea. If this kind of shift is totally impossible, don't worry: later sections will explain how to get around it.

Now let's go through the house and see what simple changes could make your home full of healing, helpful energy.

Right **Spiral staircases look fabulous, but can cause health problems in feng shui terms. If you have one, try training a green, creeping plant around the banister and install a light on the ceiling above the staircase to shine from the top floor to the bottom.**

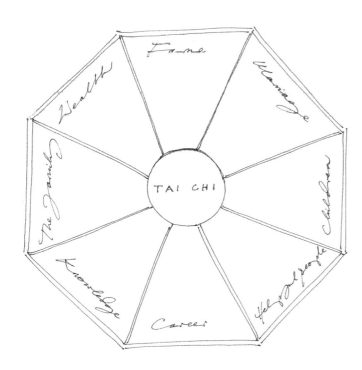

front door & the hall

Your front door is known as the 'Mouth of Chi' because it is where most of the energy will come into the house. Make sure it is smart and freshly painted: a battered-looking door will force you to fight to reach your goals; life will be a struggle and battle. Your door furniture should be bright and gleaming to attract money and luck. Now check it opens smoothly and easily: a door that sticks will bring irritations into your life and slow you down. Don't hang so many coats on your door that it won't open properly: you will be limiting your opportunities.

If your house has a number or a name it should ideally be hung at an upward slant, the end of the name higher than the beginning. You might consider giving your house a name if it doesn't already have one. Naming a house gives it even more of a character and also reflects your aims and aspirations. Choose carefully: do you want your home to reflect peace and tranquillity or prestige and power? Is it a cute, snug *The Hobbit* or a grand, serene *The White House*? Ask your house for some input. Don't forget, however, to display the number of your house clearly (if you live in a long street or apartment block) to make life easy for tradespeople and emergency services.

Either side of your front door or front gate is a wonderful place for features such as statues, ornamental pots, boulders or guardian creatures. The Chinese use Fu dogs but you can choose whatever stone guardians you like: lions maybe, dragons, hunting dogs? Heavy features like this protect the house and prevent energy from escaping. However, if you live in an area where they are more likely to be burgled, you might consider putting them in the hall (*see below*).

THE HALL

Whether it's a grand baronial hall, a long corridor or simply the space behind your door, halls are important too. If your hall or behind-the-door space is packed with boots, coats and other clutter you may find your opportunities are always limited – you are restricting the new, fresh energy coming into the house. Make sure

your hall is well-lit, bright and cheerful. It is the first place you see in your home and should be upbeat and welcoming. Make an effort by decorating it in cheerful colors; ensure the lights are all working and give it a boost with a cheery vase of flowers. Mirrors can make a dark hall look brighter and bigger.

Wind chimes by the front door are supremely good feng shui. Choose the little ones which gently tinkle rather than those huge outdoor wooden ones. They should softly ring when you enter the house but make sure the door cannot hit the chimes directly. Wind chimes sited in this way will usher in more money and keep away bad luck. A pair of guardian dogs or creatures can protect your house: think of Cerberus, the mythical dog who guards the gates of hell. Now there's a fearsome guardian who might give burglars second thoughts.

Does your hall lead straight into a long corridor? Can you see straight through to the other side of the house? Or are you looking at a series of doors in a straight line? If so the chi could race too quickly through your home. There are a few options. You could hang a heavy curtain to make the flow of energy pause, or you could hang a crystal between the doors so the energy will stop and play around the crystal before heading off. You might have the opposite problem: a dead end of a wall or a blocked-off door at the end of your hall. Try putting a mirror on it to reflect the energy back into your home.

Before you leave the hall, check it is as clear and uncluttered as possible. Hallways and corridors are considered the veins and arter-

ies of the house. Like the blood vessels of our own bodies, they need to be kept clear. And make sure that any furniture in them is soft and rounded. Sharp protruding corners provide harmful energy known as 'cutting chi'.

YOUR FIRST ROOM

What is the first room you come to? Do you walk straight into a living room or is your kitchen right there in front of you? The first rooms you see when you walk into a home will determine the life of the people who live there.

Studies, living rooms and spacious halls are the most desirable rooms to have near your entrance.

If the first room you see is a kitchen, the household will be food-orientated and will be likely to indulge in some excessive eating! Children in particular are liable to grow chubby. Not only that,

but you will find that friends are constantly dropping by to eat – fine if you're very sociable but it might be nice to have a little control, wouldn't it? If this is the case in your house, keep the kitchen door shut and hang a mirror on it.

If the first room you see is the bedroom, you will tend to be always tired. Again, a mirror fixed firmly on the door will help.

If the first room you see is the bathroom, you've got problems. The siting of bathrooms is considered crucial to feng shui. Plumbing is thought to affect two crucial areas: your finances and your health. If you are unlucky enough to have a bathroom right in front of you when you walk in, place large mirrors on all four interior walls of the bathroom to seal off the energy.

Above **The entrance to your living space is very important – it is where most of the energy will come into the house. Heavy guardian creatures at the side of the door protect the house and stop energy from leaving.**

bathrooms

Seeing as we're already talking about bathrooms, let's continue. Where is your bathroom situated on the ba-gua? If it's in your wealth area you could be flushing money down the pan! If it's in the very center of the house, the mysterious area known as the *Tai Chi* which corresponds to the very heart and soul of your home, it could affect your health. If it's in the marriage area, your relationships could be problematic. The solution in all these cases is to mirror your bathroom as before. Another problem can arise if your bathroom is at the end of a long

Left **If your bathroom is situated in a bad position in the house, use mirrors on the walls to seal off the energy. This has the added bonus of making a room look much bigger.**

Opposite **An open toilet seat spells instant financial disaster – make sure it stays closed, even if you have to put up a sign!**

corridor – again it is bad for the family's health. In one case, a woman could not have children. A feng shui expert suggested she hang a beaded curtain in the corridor to disperse the chi (a wind chime, crystal or mobile would have done the same trick) and a year later she was a happy mother. In an ideal world, the bathroom and kitchen should be well apart from each other (now you understand why feng shui is actually so practical: any public health inspector would tell you the same thing). If they are too close, in feng shui terms, any money you earn will be lost in next to no time. If there's no way you can shift the situation, always keep doors shut and put a mirror on the outside of the bathroom door. Place something heavy, a large piece of furniture such as a kitchen or dining table, between the two, closer to the kitchen.

Also make sure the bathroom is always spotlessly clean and that the toilet seat is always, ALWAYS, kept down. An open toilet seat is very bad feng shui – all your positive chi could be escaping as fast as it comes in. It also looks untidy and is not very hygenic. Men are hopeless at remembering about this so put up a notice saying 'DON'T FLUSH MONEY DOWN THE PAN – PUT THE LID DOWN!' or something like that.

bedrooms

Y ou can create a sense of happiness and wellbeing by placing your bed in the best possible position. If you cannot have your bedroom in the best spot in your house, don't worry – you can often shift your bed and create equally good results. So far we have only looked at the ba-gua in terms of the whole house, but you can super-impose the ba-gua on any single room in the house just as easily. So go into your bedroom and stand on the threshold with your back to the door. Depending on where your door lies you will be standing in either the

career (the center), helpful people (right-hand corner) or knowledge (left-hand corner). Now you can plot the rest of the ba-gua – wealth will lie off in the far left-hand corner and marriage in the far right-hand corner. Where you place your bed will depend on the age and circumstances of the person sleeping there.

CHILDREN

Children should always sleep in the children position of the room. If the bed cannot be put there, put a lamp there plus something white (flowers or a fluffy toy perhaps). Choose furniture for a child's room with care – large, heavy pieces of furniture can be harmful for a young child's chi and health. Mobiles and wind chimes are wonderful: they stimulate chi and make your child more motivated and even more intelligent! Colorful objects and fish-bowls also help. Keep colors soft and gentle for babies and very young children.

FIFTEEN TO TWENTY-TWO YEAR OLDS

People in this age group need more peace and stability in their bed-rooms. Their bed should be in the knowledge position or, if impossible, put something black, blue or green there. A plant, wind chime or crystal could also help to boost that area. Books near the entrance to the room can help their studies. If they are leaving school or college you will

need to boost the career and/or helpful people corner (more about that in the next chapter).

COUPLES

If you're in a relationship (and particularly if you're looking for one) you should make sure your bed is in the marriage position. If that is impossible, put something red in that spot – maybe some rich velvet cushions or pillows or a sumptuous crimson throw. The shape of your bed is important too: while beds with separate mattresses

Right **Emotionally volatile teenagers need bedrooms that provide peace and stability. Their bed should be in the knowledge position.**

Above **Couples should plump for a king-size bed situated in the marriage position of the room. Wherever possible move beds well away from beams and keep the head of your bed clear.**

may be supremely comfortable, they could also be divisive.

Equally, twin beds could make relationships rocky. One man whose marriage was on the rocks was advised to replace his twin beds with a king-size mattress. The cracks between the beds were representing a chasm in their relationship in energetic terms. The new bed worked a treat.

Feng shui expert Sarah Rossbach gives an unusual tip for any woman who wants to become pregnant or who is already pregnant. She suggests that beds should neither be moved, nor dusted underneath because according to the Chinese view of conception and birth the universe is full of spirits waiting to be born (known as ling). The ling are said to float under beds, waiting for the moment to enter the womb. If the bed is always being moved or cleaned, the ling might scatter, causing infertility or possibly even miscarriage.

Older people should ideally sleep in the family position. Again, if that's impossible or difficult, there is an alternative: put something green (or a wind chime or crystal) in either the wealth or fame corners.

Beams look attractive in bedrooms but can symbolize division and ill-health. If you have a beam directly above your bed running vertically down the bed it could cause difficulties in your relationship. If the beam cuts across your body horizontally, it could cause health problems: someone with a beam across the throat area may have a constant sore throat and tonsillitis. Where possible, move beds away from beams. If that is impractical, drape the beam with garlands of dried hops (they'll give you sweet dreams too) or pin soft fabric along the beam to soften the energy shooting down onto you.

Built-in cupboards or shelves around or over the bed are awkward too, causing headaches, sore throats and a feeling of being hemmed in. Keep the head of your bed as clear as possible. Bedroom furniture in general should be soft and rounded. Mirrors are not a great idea in bedrooms. They can cause insomnia or bad dreams and nightmares.

And finally, your bed should give you a clear view of the door. The ideal position for a bed is one where you can see the door clearly from your bed but not have it directly in front of you (i.e. with your feet pointing out the door). It may take some serious juggling to manage this and have your bed in the most auspicious position for your age and circumstances.

kitchens

Kitchens are considered very important in feng shui because the Chinese equate food with wealth and success. A cook should always work in a clear, brightly-lit and well-ventilated kitchen. Ideally, he or she should be able to see the door to the kitchen. The reason for this is pretty practical: if you're cooking the last thing you want is someone startling you from behind when you've got a pot of boiling water in your hand. If you can't see the door (and don't feel like getting a brand-new kitchen!) then put up a large mirror so you can see anyone coming in as

you work. Even if you don't actually need a mirror it's a great idea to put a mirror behind your stove: it symbolically doubles the number of burners, which are equated with wealth and success.

The stove is the most important piece of equipment in the kitchen, and even in the house. Interestingly, this ties in with the relevance of Hestia and how the stove was the original hearth and heart of the home. To honor the hearth your stove must be kept clean and well-working at all times. If the burners are clogged it is said you will never clear your debts. Make sure you use all the burners: the more burners you use, the more money earned. In China it is believed that if some burners are not regularly used, the family fortunes will suffer.

These are just basic guidelines but even these simple points can make a real difference in your home. Try some of them out and see what happens. Move your bed and you could find you sleep better, your baby sleeps through the night, or even that you end up sharing your bed with someone new and wonderful. Boost your kitchen with a few mirrors and a few cheques might come through the post. Keep that hallway clean and bright and new opportunities might appear as if by magic. In the next chapter we'll take it all one stage further...

Right **The position of this stove is ideal in feng shui terms, as the cook has freedom of movement and is able to see anyone approaching from the outside.**
Far right **It may be difficult to arrange a small galley kitchen ideally but you can always add a mirror and keep your stove clean.**

USING THE CURES

There are several ways you can bring a missing area back into your home. Which one you choose will depend very much on your circumstances and the physical practicalities of your space.

Hops hung over beams are thought to have the effect of softening their cutting chi. They may even usher in good fortune.

If you own the whole house and also the land around it, you have several options. If you really wanted to splash out, you could extend your house – or add a conservatory, but that's a pretty drastic and wildly expensive option. Another solution is to bring the corner in with light. External lights are sited so they illuminate the 'left-out' area. If you don't want bright lights outside then try using one of the 'heavy things' cures. 'Square off' your corner, figuring where the actual corner would be were it to exist. Then place a large, solid, heavy object in that corner. See what fits – it could be a big beautiful statue, a heavy urn, or a big terracotta pot with a wonderfully healthy plant in it (two cures for the price of one).

If you live in an apartment or don't own the land outside you can still square off your missing corner using mirrors. Simply place mirrors along the walls which edge your missing area. This will work just as well.

USING THE CURES TO SOLVE OTHER PROBLEMS

The list of problems the cures can help is never-ending. The following list outlines just a few. If your particular problem is not on the list, check out the feng shui titles given in the Bibliography – or splash out and treat yourself and your house to a feng shui consultation.

Spiral staircases look lovely but can cause health problems, particularly if they are in the center of the house. Wrap a vine or green twining plant (a creeper or ivy) around the handle or banister. Install a light on the ceiling above the staircase to shine from the top floor down to the bottom.

Beams over the stove in your kitchen are as tricky as beams in your bedroom. Any money you lend is unlikely to be returned. Put bamboo flutes over the beam (*see drawing*) or hang a piece of red fringing along the edge of the beam.

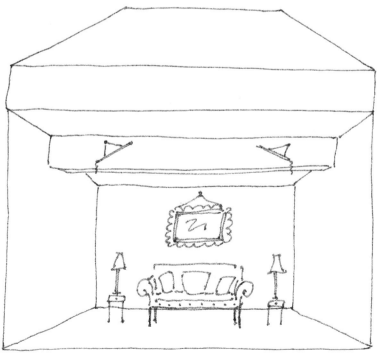

Above **Bamboo flutes offset the damaging chi of a beam.**

If a door is overly large, too much chi will enter, creating disturbing energy and possibly dispersing cash. Install a wind chime as a cure in the front hall. Also put a heavy object (a statue or large attractive stone perhaps) at the entrance near the door. Two large stone urns either side of the door can create a steadying effect too. If your door is too small, on the other hand, place a mirror on the top or on the sides of the door to give the effect of height and width.

Right **Placing a mirror on a blank, dead-end wall at the end of a corridor makes good feng shui sense, but if it is placed too high it will only serve to make people feel uncomfortable.**

In a house, doors represent parents' mouths while the windows represent children's voices. If the windows in your home outnumber the doors by three to one or over, there will be constant arguing. Children will be cheeky and always talking back. The cure is to hang a bell or wind chime near the door – the idea is that, when it opens, its stern parental voice will be heard by the windows, pulling them back into line.

Check your front and back doors. If they lie in a direct straight line (i.e. you can see right through them both when they're open), you could find it hard to hold on to cash. Place a plant in between the two doors or, even more effectively, hang a small spherical crystal on a string so it hangs below the level of the doors: this causes the chi to pause and circulate around the house rather than rushing straight in and out.

Look through your windows and check the view. If you have a road coming directly at your home, the best cure is to put a mirror on your front door or gate to deflect the chi. It needn't be large: you could find a ba-gua mirror in Chinese shops or choose a small circular mirror which will look attractive. If you have a church or large building in sight of any window, put up either a small silver ball (one of the Mayan bell balls is great) on a red string or a ba-gua mirror in the window. This will deflect the oppressive 'cutting' chi sent from the building.

This part of the book has, it is hoped, given you some idea of the fundamentals of feng shui, how it works, and how you can apply it to your home. We'll look at how feng shui can be used to boost particular areas to achieve specific results in the final part of the book. But for now, it's time to leave feng shui to do its arcane and wonderful business while we shift our emphasis and prepare to indulge our senses in Part Five.

PART 5

the
sensual
home

color as therapy

a truly healing home, a home of the spirit, should delight all the senses. So far we have worked very hard: figuring out what we want from our homes; cleaning, clearing and adjusting the energy. Now it's time to have some fun. This next section is all about simple ways to turn your home into a space which is truly inviting, alluring and enticing: a place which thrills the eye, gladdens the ear and delights the nose; a place full of things which beg to be touched and stroked. We are entering the world of Aphrodite, the goddess not just of love, but of beauty and

all things that please the eye and delight the senses as well. Social psychologist Ginette Paris believes that the absence of beauty, the ignorance of Aphrodite, can lead to depression, so let's not neglect the beautiful and joy-bringing goddess in our home. We'll start our sensual odyssey with a look at the intriguing and beguiling world of color.

> *Modern psychology does not seem to have given much recognition to the pathogenic character of an 'ugly' environment, that is, an environment in which Aphrodite is not honored in any form.*
>
> Ginette Paris, Psychologist

Color has the power to lift our spirits; to soothe our souls; to enliven us or calm us: it is the supreme mood shifter. So by bringing color into our homes we can subtly but very effectively change the atmosphere of the house and the feelings of those who live in it. Color has been used for millennia to shift the emotions and heal illness, and modern research bears out the ancient wisdom.

Never underestimate the power of color in your home. Even if you don't consider yourself a very visual person, you will still be affected because our whole bodies are sensitive to it; we don't just 'see' color with our eyes, we feel it and sense it as well. Numerous

experiments have shown that most people can actually 'feel' color with their fingertips when blindfolded. So no wonder the colors we choose for our homes can have enormous effects on our lives.

TRANSFORMING THE HOME WITH COLOR

The wonderful thing about color is that it offers one of the quickest, most satisfying ways of completely changing the mood of a room – or an entire house. Slapping on a fresh coat of paint is quick and cheap. You can transform a cold, unwelcoming dining room into a warm, sensual feasting parlor with a judicious coat of lip-smacking vermilion. A dingy urban living room can echo the shimmer of spring in the country with a cool fresh green. The softest mauve ushers a sense of peace and spirituality into a meditation or healing space; a buttercup yellow makes a kitchen a friendly, welcoming place where everyone wants to meet and eat. And the beauty of it is that if you don't like the effect you've created, then you can simply paint it out and start afresh.

If you don't have the time or the inclination, you don't even need to go to all the trouble and expense of completely redecorating. Sometimes all a room cries out for is the addition of a few accent colors: deep-red and pink cushions to make a lack-lustre bedroom an exotic boudoir; solid dark-green lamps to earth a rather fey pink drawing room; splashes of vivid blues, reds or yellows to lift a plain white hall.

Left **Bold use of color almost always pays off – here, the bright orange old-fashioned telephone beautifully sets off the vivid pink of the kitchen cupboards, creating warmth and atmosphere.**

Unfortunately, most of us tend to be rather scared of color and imagine that nobody except a trained interior designer could dare to mix and match anything other than the safest hues. So we stick to the tried and trusted and haul home gallons of plain white, ubiquitous magnolia, and the palest, safest pastel shades that the local store has to offer. If you feel happy with these, fine. But if, deep inside, you feel you'd really like to try something a little more adventurous then perhaps it is time to start educating your sense of color.

Begin with nature, that superb teacher. Look around you and pick out the colors that really make your soul sing. Flowers make a wonderful palette; so do the kaleidoscope of russet, gold and ochre leaves in the autumn. Catch the pure blue of a summer sky and compare it with the blues of sea, lakes, pools – and then with the myriad blues of flowers, from the soft haze of bluebells to the clear tones of a delphinium.

But which colors might work in your home? Which combinations could be most effective? Sometimes nature does something so surprising that you would never have thought of it in a million years: it mixes colors in such a subtle or startling way you can find endless inspiration if you just teach yourself to really open your eyes and look around you at the natural world.

Now take yourself 'window-shopping'. Stock up on color charts from paint manufacturers – build up a library of colors. Go around the fabric counters of the large stores – not just furnishing fabrics but dressmaking fabrics too. Take a trip to your local art shop and pick out the paints you adore: tubes of gouache come in wonderful vibrant colors.

Above **If your tastes tend to be rather traditional, and you have never ventured into the world of color before, take time to look around you before making any changes.**

Now take your colorful trawl home and play with it. Which are your favorite colors? What effects do they have on you? What emotions do they bring to mind? Try to imagine decorating one room in a series of colors: how would it change if you swathed it in, say, forest green and then lime green; a soft ochre or a shocking pink; a rich crimson or a washed peach? How would the color changes affect the mood of the room?

finding your soul colors

I ook at the rooms in your home. Sit down and think exactly what mood you would like to create in your space. Do you want your living room to be a soothing, calming refuge or a bright, lively place to entertain friends? Look back over your notes from the earlier chapters and try to envisage how color could help those aims. Remember what it was you loved about those homes from foreign lands. Flick through your journal of cuttings and see which colors keep repeating themselves. Are you drawn to the pale winter tones of Gustavian interiors or the warm vibrant hues of a Provençal farmhouse? Does your soul chime with the muted serenity of Shaker style or clamor for the pinks and turquoises of a Caribbean hideaway? It could be any of them, or all of them. There is no rule that says you have to color your home in one style throughout. It's OK to be a tad conservative in the general 'public' areas of the house but go completely wild in bathrooms. Or you could always keep your bedroom pretty calm and serene but insist on having a bright-yellow kitchen to keep your spirits (and those of guests) cheery.

Play with color, have fun with it, experiment. There are no rules other than those you impose on yourself. Sometimes the best results come about through happy accidents. Try out surprising color schemes – see what pleases your eye. As a general rule, if you want to make a room cool choose colors with shorter wavelengths (blue, green and violet tones); if you want to make it warmer go for those with longer wavelengths (red, orange and yellow and all the colors in between). If you feel a room is too cool, introduce a balancing warm color somewhere – maybe a rug, trimmings, a throw, pictures, ornaments, pillows and cushions. And vice versa. But, above all, just play.

If you are still not feeling too confident of your intuition and sense of color, consider the following. Remember that within each color there are thousands of different shades and tones so you don't need to confine yourself to the primaries or plain pastels.

Left **Warm, burnt orange is a wonderful color for large expanses of wall. Reminiscent of Etruscan vases, it is a color full of confidence and sociability, an excellent backdrop for parties as it tends to wake people up and make them want to dance.**

THE POWER OF COLOR

These are the main attributes of the various colors.

RED

Red is associated with power, passion, energy and challenge. It's the color of fire and can increase your pulse, respiration and brain activity. It will keep you alert but can be oppressive and tiring if you stay in an intensely red room for too long. So red is ideal for rooms with lots of activity and can give warmth and interest to dark passages and cloakrooms. It makes a room look smaller and more intimate so can work well for dining rooms.

Color therapists use red for those suffering from anaemia, depression, lethargy and tiredness and any 'cold' diseases such as rheumatism and bad circulation. It's not a great color to choose for studies, except in accent colors or very soft pale rose tones. The same goes for bedrooms where a few well-chosen touches of red can raise the temperature and help create a sexy atmosphere, but too much would be overpowering. However, a red bathroom or toilet can be a really stunning success (and apparently will help ease constipation too!) Use red tones to lift a room which feels cold – add a rich warm paisley throw, crimson lampshades or a vibrant Persian rug or kilim.

Tone red down and you end up with pink which can, if you're not careful, end up looking sickly or plain bland. But team the brighter, gutsier pinks with cool white walls and natural flooring and you could be on to a winner. Pink also works well with sage greens. And, if you really want to make a bold statement, go for the shocking pink of silks and saris – for a bedspread, blind or a few glamorous cushions or pillows.

ORANGE

Orange is the color of confidence, of joy and sociability. It stimulates the appetite and reduces tiredness and fatigue. Therapeutically, it is used for stimulating the immune system, for reducing pain, healing gout, gallstones, ulcers, depression, constipation and alcoholism. It works wonderfully in dining rooms, corridors, living rooms and anywhere you like to entertain and be sociable. It stimulates joyfulness, release of emotions and is wonderful for parties as it encourages movement and dancing.

Don't shudder at the thought of pure-orange orange; there are a host of tones. Think of Etruscan vases and Italian frescoes; dusty,

dusky, yellowy oranges can look wonderful. As with red, this isn't the best color to pick for bedrooms except as an accent. And don't put orange tones near black as together they draw out all the warmth and emotion and can leave you feeling deprived and miserable.

Above **The palest tones of cream and gray can impart a very calm, restful atmosphere to a room and particularly suite the graceful, sweeping shapes and heady angles of some modern architecture.**

YELLOW

Yellow is pure sunlight and it does everything sunlight can do: it lifts the spirits, banishes depression and raises your energy levels. It's great for self-esteem and can really boost your ego. Yellow can be a good friend if you're studying as it sharpens the memory, and can work wonders in a home office as it stimulates the left side of the brain which governs judgment, logic and reasoning.

There are hoards of yellows – from pure primrose through jaunty buttercup to sophisticated mustard shades. Color thera-

pists use it to help heal arthritis, jaundice, stiffness and immobility, depression, skin problems and mental tiredness. Yellow works well in most 'downstairs' rooms – kitchens, halls, living rooms, playrooms, games rooms, studies. It will cheer up almost any room, particularly if you team it with soft creamy colors and remember that blue looks great with yellow too. Yellow can be a bit too energetic for bedrooms, like its cousins orange and red. It's wonderful to wake up to but not so good for drifting off to sleep with.

GREEN

Green is the color of nature and sits exactly in the middle of the color spectrum. Our eye muscles don't need to adjust to green so it is a color which can bring harmony, contentment and calm. It soothes all the senses and fosters equilibrium; it's a reassuring

color. Color therapists use it to ease migraines and tension headaches, moodiness, stress, gastric ulcers, digestive upsets, anxiety and all agitated emotional states. It can stimulate fertility and ease the heart, blood and circulation. Green encourages balanced judgment and is very helpful for teenagers and anyone with troubled emotions.

Green can be a little too cool for many people but works well in living rooms when softened by warmer shades such as dusky pinks or apricots. It can also give a balancing touch of coolness in that sensual red dining room – how about trying a rich green tartan fabric to offset the red? And don't think greens need to be sage and boring: lime green is far from safe.

Above **The deeper shades of green work well in formal dining rooms when a touch of elegance is called for. A red-shaded lamp provides the perfect warming balance.**

BLUE

Blue, the color of the sky and of the sea, is supremely restful and soothing. Imagine a cool mountain stream running through smooth rocks, or staring up at a perfectly clear blue sky. It helps you relax and switch off but can also make communication clear and effective. Blue focuses the mind and the intellect. In therapy it's used to help lower blood pressure, heart rate and respiration. It calms the central nervous system and can reduce stress. It's also used for itching, toothache, hernias, back problems and muscular aches and pains.

Blue is a perfect color for bedrooms, home studies and looks great in bathrooms too. Think about turquoise as well – a clear chiming tone which can lift a bathroom and makes a surprising but effective choice for kitchens. You may well find you need something warmer to balance blue – yellow and warm browns work well.

INDIGO

Shades of indigo are said to enhance psychic powers, to promote day-dreaming and to restore your balance with the outside world. In therapy it is used to treat obsessions and all forms of emotional instability. Soft indigo shades could be perfect for a private retreat room or healing space. It would work well, too, for a peaceful bedroom. It is also known as 'midnight blue', and some experts say it can encourage introversion so don't use it too widely. However, a shot of sheer indigo can make a striking accent color: look out for sheer clear silks and sumptuous velvets in this unusual color.

VIOLET

Violet calms the spirit at the deepest level. It also soothes both body and mind. Gentle, soft violet is also considered the most spiritual color so is often chosen for meditation rooms, sick rooms and healing spaces. Therapists use violet for skin conditions, insomnia, tension and oversensitivity. Not everyone feels comfortable with violet shades but think about soft lilac, lavender and foxglove; the soft blue-violet of hyacinth. All these can be delightful in bedrooms and will make guests feel an instant sense of peace and tranquillity if used in their rooms. Also think about introducing touches of violet and mauve into other rooms – a soft violet sofa could look wonderful against creamy yellow walls; pale peppermint green also acts as a good foil.

BLACK

Black heightens our emotional response but is very oppressive if used as a solid color. Use black accessories, such as picture frames, lamp-bases, tie-backs, to highlight areas of a room. It can help give body to a wishy-washy color scheme and can endow a living or dining room with added drama. All-black rooms, however, are strictly for that brief (hopefully) phase of teenage rebellion!

WHITE

White is clean and calming but can be very stark. It can be useful for meditation or when your senses feel overloaded but most people don't feel comfortable living with pure white for too long. It suggests purity but can leach away the warmth and experience of living. However, if you break it up with the odd burst of color it can be very soothing and effective. Having said that, there are many shades of white. If you use toning shades of white – egg white; bone white; milk white or the softer, creamier tones of oatmeal, calico, straw and wax white – you can create a simple yet sophisticated effect.

And don't forget the bliss of white accessories: pure-white linen on a guest bed simply invites slumber. A milk bottle brimming with white daisies; an elegant vase full of lilies; an enamel jug stuffed with cow parsley. Pure-white china or creamy earthenware looks stunning against a colorful kitchen. Sumptuous white towels and bathrobes are the perfect foil to a turquoise bathroom. Gauzy white drapes make any color scheme softer and fresher.

BROWN

Much despised over recent years as a decorating color, brown is making a comeback. It's the color of the rich loamy earth; the myriad shades of a tree's bark; the chestnut or bay gloss of a horse's coat; the brindle of a dog; the tortoiseshell of a cat. The darker browns can be a bit gloomy as an overall shade (with the exception of wooden panelling) but they look wonderful as accent colors, giving a similar, but softer and more organic, emphasis than black.

Wood is the obvious way to bring in brown – rich mahogany tones lift a dull color scheme; soft oak gives warmth; cool ash and beech give light. Think too of the inviting familiarity of a battered leather sofa; the sumptuous texture of suede; a comfortable armchair upholstered in warm brown corduroy or velour. And when you soften brown down to creamier tones such as clay, brick and milk chocolate, brown can be soothing, comforting and very chic.

OTHER THOUGHTS ON COLOR

Once you start thinking about color, you will notice it everywhere and come up with a thousand different ways to entice it into your home. But here are a few ideas to get you started:

Introduce colored glass into your home. It doesn't need to be a whole window: maybe just a panel. Or hang a piece of stained glass in a window to catch the light. There are also stickers which give a stained-glass effect (although they are never quite as pellucid). If you have a collection of colored bottles, glass or vases, display them against the light: on a window ledge or build a shelf to span a window and watch the colors come to life.

Let rainbows dance around your home by hanging multi-faceted crystals in windows and doors where they will catch the sunshine. Experiment with different sizes and shapes: those with wider, larger edges will send out bands of deep rainbow light; those with more smaller facets will beam out smaller dancing shimmers of color. Children adore them (and often think they are dancing fairies) cats will spend endless happy hours trying to catch the beautiful rainbow creatures.

You don't need loads of money. If you fancy a simple change of style for next to nothing, buy a roll of cheap muslin or calico and dye it yourself. Fabric dyes are easy to use and cheap to buy and they come in a huge array of sumptuous colors. Use the material to make curtains; to cover furniture; to create 'secret' areas by hanging lengths from the ceiling; to create an exotic Arabian Nights bed (billowing folds of several shades of the desert). Pin it up to cover uneven walls. If you're really feeling creative, add stencilled or free-hand designs or pictures.

Painting junk furniture can also be great fun – and brings a splash of color into any room. There are now hordes of books and courses teaching you how to do it yourself. You can achieve pretty well any effect you like: from a distressed country farmhouse look on a kitchen dresser to a bright jungle scene on a child's toy chest. Can't paint? Try decoupage – decorating a surface with cut-out pictures or designs – it couldn't be easier, and creates amazing effects for little outlay.

Relearn the old childhood art of papier-mâché. With a pile of old newspaper and a tub of paste you can make incredible decorative bowls, plates and dishes. Add chicken wire and the sky's the limit: you could make mock Grecian urns, or Romanesque statues, Corinthian columns or a whole zoo of animals. Paint them as restrained or as wild as you like.

Plants and flowers are obvious ways to bring in a splash of color and can be a great way to try out new color schemes before committing them to paint or fabric. A vase of one-colored flowers can give you a great idea of how a color will work. The kinds of flowers you are drawn to will also give you a taste of the colors you truly love, but might not dare to think of for decorating! But buy them for sheer fun too. Pick the ones that suit your mood or simply beg to be bought: a bunch of soft, old-fashioned roses in dusty pinks and cream or a spray of brightly colored daisy-like gerberas screaming 'look at us!'

Who said plants have to be displayed in boring pots or clear glass vases? Terracotta pots bring warmth to cold color schemes and can work well but there's nothing written in stone (or terracotta) to say they have to stay that color. Paint them any shade you choose – or use several toning or clashing shades in any one room. Think laterally for other receptacles for plants and flowers: in

a taste of tequila

There are a million unusual ways to introduce splashes of color into every room in your home without decorating.

- You could turn a boring kitchen into a vibrant slice of Mexico simply by picking out gaudily colored buckets, bowls, tea towels and utensils.
- Throw a rug down on the floor, chuck a screaming loud cloth over the table and you're halfway to Tequila.
- String up some plastic chillies – even better, find a string of lights covered with chillies or other bright fruit and festoon them around a chandelier – or a home-made one fashioned out of coat-hangers or chicken wire.
- Use your journal; look at travel books and magazines, not just interior design tomes – and let your imagination run riot.

Greece they often plant geraniums and other plants in brightly-colored tins – either left with their original marketing message or whitewashed for a dash of Aegean chic.

Bathrooms are often neglected color orphans. Brighten them up by collecting soaps in different colors – the translucent ones are best; they look like gorgeous edible jellies. Bath potions now come in a host of scrumptious colors and beautiful containers – decant them into pretty bottles and display them with a light behind them to catch the gleam of their tones. If you're still too nervous about using vivid colors in paint or fabrics, pick out some really wild towels.

Introduce color in your lighting as well as your furnishings and details. Experiment with colored lightbulbs and colored cellophane over the light fitting. Red lights enhance activity and could also bring some added spice to the bedroom! Orange lights can get a party going as they stimulate appetite and get everybody up on the dance floor. Yellow could be handy if you're studying for an exam. Blue lights are restful, while green bulbs restore balance and harmony – although both can be rather cold and a little gloomy if you're not careful.

Color therapists often use colored lights to shine into baths. You can have a therapeutic colored bath in your own home by adding natural food dyes to the water. Red will invigorate, blue will relax, green will balance and yellow will be cheery – or simply follow your mood. You can even change your color halfway through by adding another primary color: blue and yellow will make green; red and yellow will go orange; blue and red will turn purple. Complete the scene by surrounding your bath with colored candles. Note: don't use artificial colorings as most of them contain unpleasant chemicals.

Make mealtimes a colorful affair by choosing food with attractive colors. You could play with themed color meals: shades of green maybe; or an orange feast. Natural food colorings can help too. Or go for the most colorful you can find – decorate salads with edible flowers such as borage and nasturtium; garnish ice-creams with lavender and rose petals; polish off almost anything with a symphony of green herbs. Or be very exotic and try startling combinations such as coral-pink scallops on black squid-

ink pasta. One tip: sadly all-white meals don't look stylish: they just look bland!

Update a room instantly by adding loose covers to chairs and tables. You could make them yourself (some are incredibly easy) or find a local stitcher. If you pick cheap fabrics you can ring the changes with every season – or every passing whim. Your dining room could shift from the clean, crisp lines of blue and white ticking through sophisticated damask to wild jungle print. The same goes for blinds and curtains: why stick with the same design for years when you're longing for a change? In the olden days housewives had 'winter' and 'summer' curtains. If you choose cheaper fabrics you could have as many as suit your mood.

Right **Hanging mirrors or pieces of furniture with strings of fairly lights or multifaceted glass baubles that reflect the light is another ingenious way of introducing color into your home.**

the scented home

Often the very first thing you will notice about a house is its scent. Not how it looks; not how fashionable the furniture is but how it smells. Our noses are incredibly sensitive and how we feel about a place will undoubtedly be affected by how our sense of smell perceives it. So what greets you as you walk into your abode? Does the place smell warm and inviting with perhaps the light scent of lavender floor polish, a hint of pot pourri and the wafting pleasure of a vase of heady roses? Or maybe it smells clean and fresh, with the merest accent of pine needles or the brisk energy of a citrus tang? Then again, perhaps it smells musty and dusty (hopefully not after all that cleaning!) or gives off the rather pungent scent of old trainers and sports kit? Or are you greeted by stale cooking smells – the lingering scent of chicken or cabbage?

> The first thing to greet your guests as they enter your home is the aroma, and the impression it creates may be more enduring than that made by the fixtures and fittings.
>
> Valerie Ann Worwood, *The Fragrant Pharmacy*

The ancient Greeks believed that beautiful scents were a means of contacting the gods. They possessed an entire language of perfumery in which flowery scents were chosen to invoke peace, joy or even pure sensuality. So, if you want to make your home into a truly delicious haven for the senses, indulge your nostrils. Filling your home with carefully chosen scents can uplift the emotions, fill your body with energy or repose and seduce your soul with sheer delight. Scent is a powerful but also infinitely subtle way of shifting the atmosphere in your home. Get it right and you can regulate, not just your own mood, but that of your family, friends and any casual visitors as well. Now that's tantamount to magic.

There are a host of simple ways to bring delicious scents into every room of the house. But whatever you do, please don't race out and stock up on a bunch of synthetic air fresheners, odor-eaters and fake scent-inducers. First of all, synthetic smells will always smell synthetic. There is something faintly sickly and unreal about them. Secondly, many people find they are allergic to synthetic perfumes – they are a common cause of allergic reactions and will undoubtedly cause problems for anyone prone to asthma, eczema, hayfever and so on. Thirdly, aerosols containing chlorofluorocarbons (CRCs) pollute the environment by damaging the ozone layer and can be detrimental to our own health by irritating the lungs and mucous membranes. These should be enough reasons to give them a wide berth.

Turn instead to natural fragrances – flowers, herbs, aromatherapy oils, fruit. These are the tools of the goddess Aphrodite who reigns over the scents, not just of love, but of pleasure, happiness and delight too. It's well worth paying her a little homage in this sweet-scented way.

Our ancestors certainly venerated Aphrodite by keeping the home smelling sweet naturally – sweet-fragranced herbs such as lavender and woodruff were strewn on the floors or under mats to release their perfume as guests walked over them; nosegays of oranges and spices hung in kitchens; herbs were used to keep laundry smelling fresh and to deter moths and bugs. We can take some tips from their examples. Fortunately there is a really simple shortcut – aromatherapy.

USING ESSENTIAL OILS IN THE HOME

The essential oils of aromatherapy are the simplest way to make your home smell wonderful all year round. It doesn't take long to learn how to use the oils – the only part that tends to take time is choosing which to use. They all smell so wonderful you will be hard-pushed to make the decision.

There are just a few ground rules before starting this sybaritic process. Firstly, make sure you choose oils which are pure (some cheap brands will dilute the essential oil with a base oil; some so-called 'aromatherapy' oils even use synthetic scents). Basically, true essential oils are purely natural. The essence of a plant's perfume, they are obtained from the leaves, petals, bark and seeds of the plant or fruit from which they are derived. Buy from a reputable health shop and check the label for added ingredients. True oils will vary greatly in price depending on the oil you choose, so if all the oils are around the same price or if you're offered rose or neroli oil very cheaply then you can be sure it's not the real thing.

Secondly, you should be aware that although aromatherapy is a wonderful healing art, essential oils are powerful substances which should be used with great respect. Many can be highly toxic if swallowed and some people are allergic to them. Never use more than the stated amounts; never take them internally and never put them straight on to your skin without the advice of a qualified aromatherapist. There are certain oils that should not be used during pregnancy: these include sage, pennyroyal, basil, oregano, fennel, hyssop, juniper, myrrh, rosemary and clary sage, but always check with a qualified professional before you use any oil in pregnancy. Those with health problems should also use caution and consult a professional before using the oils.

If you are prone to allergies, try a spot test before you use any of the mixtures – put a tiny amount of the finished product on your inner arm and leave it for 24 hours. If you have any allergic reactions do not use the potion. You can test individual oils in the same way by diluting them in a little base oil (such as sweet almond) and applying as before (although, just to make life really difficult, some people are also allergic to sweet almond oil!) If you are very sensitive you will just have to try the recipes on the following pages with great care and not be too disappointed if they set you sneezing: there are alternatives you can use which don't use essential oils: you will learn more about these later on.

Above **Nothing can beat the scent of freshly picked flowers as you walk into a room. By using aromatherapy, the heady scents of a dozen different blooms can be with us every day.**

AROMATHERAPY IDEAS

There are many ways of using essential oils in the home. These are the most common.

- You can buy special oil burners and diffusers. Generally, the burner will have a reservoir in which you place first water and then a few drops of your chosen oil or oils; underneath is a place for a night-light which gently heats the water and releases the oil. Remember to keep the water topped up or you will end up with a sticky mess of oil which is fiendishly difficult to remove. Diffusers are usually plugged into the mains and have strips or pads which are soaked with oils: sometimes they are linked with an ionizer.
- For a shorter-lasting scent, put a few drops of oil in a bowl of warm water. The scent will not last as long as the burners and diffusers but can work well for parties, dinners or in sick rooms.
- You can also buy special rings to put directly onto light bulbs. You simply add a few drops of oil to the ring and they gently scent the room.
- Make your own mist spray to replace aerosol air fresheners by filling a house plant mister with purified water and then adding essential oil. Generally speaking, you should add around 15–20 drops of oil to every 125ml (4 fl oz) of water. You will need to shake the mister before you use it to disperse the oil in the water.
- Scented candles are a lovely idea. You can buy ready-scented aromatherapy candles (again make sure they are pure aromatherapy oils and not synthetics). To be brutally honest, they are far more effective than many of the methods for scenting plain ones. If you make your own candles, then great: add around 10 drops of oil as the wax is starting to cool. If not then try this method: light the candle and wait for the wax to melt around the wick. Then blow out the flame and add a few drops of oil to the molten wax. Then relight. It won't be a strong scent but is nice on a desk or table if you're working. Don't be tempted to add more oil when the candle is alight.

THE OILS TO CHOOSE

Really, the choice of oils is totally up to you and your nose. But certain oils do have the ability to impart a particular mood to the house and to the people in it. So here's a rundown of some of the real aromatic superstars:

Relaxing oils These are the soothers and pacifiers; oils to use when you want to stop the world and float away: chamomile, clary sage, frankincense, jasmine, lavender, marjoram, melissa, neroli, rose.

Calming, reassuring oils When you're feeling anxious or apprehensive, fill your home with reassuring scents such as geranium, jasmine, lavender, melissa, neroli, palmarosa and ylang ylang.

Mind-sharpening oils Very useful when you're studying or need to keep your brain in gear. Rosemary is absolutely wonderful to keep burning while you work, followed by basil, lemon, tea tree, peppermint and pine.

Uplifting oils If you're feeling down and depressed or swamped by negativity, summon up the energy to put some of these oils into action: bergamot (a serious friend in need), chamomile, hyssop, lavender, orange and yarrow.

Pacifying oils Before you bite someone's head off because you're so irritable and angry, have a sniff of these: bergamot, chamomile, grapefruit, lavender, mandarin, orange, rose.

Morale-boosting oils When your self-esteem starts to plunge or you're faced with the quivering bottom lip of a child lacking in self-confidence, try these oils. Rosemary helps you pull yourself together; pine helps you put on a brave face. Try also cedarwood, jasmine, juniper, rose, thyme.

Energizing oils If the whole house feels slumped in torpor, wake it up with these: basil, eucalyptus, grapefruit, juniper, orange, peppermint, pine, rosemary.

Party oils Holding a party and want it to go with a swing? Jasmine is the great welcomer; geranium is a brilliantly friendly oil.

Try also a little coriander, cypress, juniper, mandarin, orange, pine, tuberose and ylang ylang.

Sensual oils Ideal for the bedroom or the great seduction scene! Go for a heady brew chosen from jasmine, rose, sandalwood, tuberose, ylang ylang.

Serene oils Perfect for meditation or for when you need to switch off and turn inwards: chamomile, frankincense, juniper, linden blossom, rose, sandalwood, vetiver.

Sickroom oils Keep the bugs away with a brew of some of these oils: eucalyptus, pine, rosemary, tea tree. Add some lavender to soothe the invalid.

House-selling oils A few drops of clary sage or lemon oils will put house viewers at ease and make them feel the house has a soft, relaxed atmosphere.

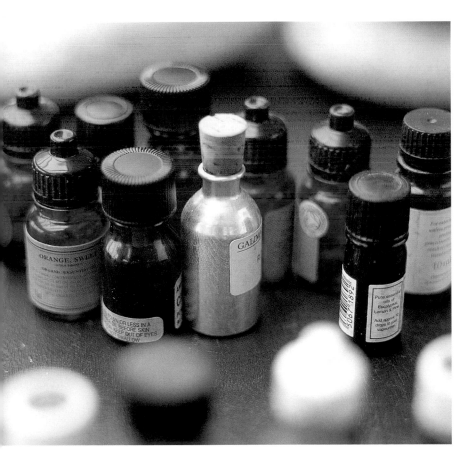

Left **Keep a variety of your favorite oils by the bath so you can use the one that suits your mood. Try making your own potions to relax or invigorate.**

Above **The bathroom should be a real sanctuary – a place where you can relax, unwind and indulge your senses in complete privacy whenever you feel the need.**

FURTHER TIPS FOR THE FRAGRANT HOME

Once you start getting into the sense of smell, it can be hard to stop. Here are a few other ideas to fragrance the home.

Ask any estate agent what scents help to sell a house and they will all say the same: freshly baked bread or cakes and freshly ground coffee beans. You don't need to be selling your home to benefit. Bak-

ing bread is therapy in its own right and knocks the spots off any shop-bought loaf. Now bread machines make it so easy there's no excuse. Set the timer before you go to bed and wake up to the delicious scent of a home bakery – and fresh warm rolls for breakfast.

Flowers are the most subtle and absolutely the most beautiful way to introduce scent into the home. Work out which flowery scents you particularly like (everyone is different) and then fill your home with the aroma of carnations, freesias, gardenias, hyacinths, jasmine, lilac, lilies, lily of the valley, mimosa, narcissi, primroses, roses (of course), scented geraniums, stocks, sweet peas, tuberose and violets. Plant sweet-smelling flowers and shrubs close to your windows so the scent wafts through: lilac, jasmine, honeysuckle, roses, night-scented stocks, wallflowers, lavender, mignonette, mock orange, heliotrope and so on.

Herbs are sweet-smelling too: fill a window-box with them or have pots around the house. The following give off the nicest scents: bergamot, lavender, lemon balm, lemon verbena, mint, rosemary, sage, southernwood, sweet woodruff and thyme.

Use natural wood and allow its resinous scent to permeate the house. If your wood is old and long past its resinous days, give it a helping hand with a few drops of essential oil – cedarwood, cypress, sandalwood, pine or rosewood rubbed under a table or chair will give a soft, subtle sense of wellbeing. Those woody oils can also add a delicious scent to logs if you have an open fire. Rub a few drops onto your logs before burning and be wafted to the exotic East or a far Northern pine forest. Don't throw out old dry herbs either – toss them onto the embers and they will scent your whole room.

In the summer, spread delicious scents around the whole garden by finishing off your barbecue by throwing on bunches of dried or fresh herbs – old lavender smells gorgeous and will add to the mellow feel of garden parties.

Make your own smudge sticks by drying lavender, sage and sweetgrass and then binding them tightly together with brightly colored cotton or thin strips of hide. Light the end and fan to get up a good smolder; then waft the sweet-smelling smoke around your whole home. Smudge sticks are used for space clearing by Native Americans and are very effective. You can use them in the space-clearing exercises given on page 88.

Fresh flowers make a house look good and well cared for. What's more, if you choose the right blooms they will keep it smelling sweet for days.

The smell of freshly brewed coffee is famous the world over for selling houses. Team it with a bowl of fresh, ripe oranges for an aroma so delicious and powerful, you can almost taste it.

ding with lavender bags – your guests will never want to leave.

Try using essential oils in the laundry room – not just to scent your clothes but to let the perfume waft right through the house too. Add three to five drops of oil to the softener compartment of the washing machine: lavender, orange blossom and chamomile are great for bed linen or bedclothes; ylang-ylang is pretty exotic and sensual; if there is a cold or flu going around, choose eucalyptus, pine or rosemary. You can tumble-dry clothes with scent by putting two drops of oil onto a handkerchief-sized piece of fabric and adding it to the load: lavender, rosemary, geranium, rosewood, jasmine and ylang-ylang all work well. For more ideas seek out Valerie Anne Worwood's books *The Fragrant Pharmacy*, *The Fragrant Mind* and *Fragrant Sensuality* (see Bibliography).

Pick bunches of fresh herbs from the garden and hang in bunches over the kitchen table to dry – the scent is subtle, they look delightful and they keep away the bugs into the bargain.

Incense is not to everyone's taste (or rather smell) but it's worth experimenting to find one you like. Heavy scents like patchouli and musk can be a bit overpowering, and some flowered scents smell very sickly and synthetic. Vanilla, however, can be a success and sandalwood works well too. Hand-blended incense – the kind you burn on a block of charcoal rather than in sticks – can be far more intense and interesting, if you can find it. Some mystical shops sell incenses which promise everything bar doing the cleaning: from summoning wealth to calling up spirits! Tibetan, Chinese and ayurvedic incenses, if you can find them, often have healing properties and can help balance the elements in your body. Try them out.

Cheer yourself up as you do the washing-up by adding a few drops of your favorite essential oil to your usual liquid. Try adding 5 drops of lime, 3 drops of bergamot, 2 drops of lavender and 1 drop of orange. Shake it all up, wash and go. The bergamot is cheering, the citrus fruits uplifting and the lavender calming.

Make your own scented drawer liners by spraying simple lining paper with your plant mister oil spray. Try cedarwood, lavender, geranium, vetiver or lemon. Put the scented side down and fill the drawer with clothes. Top up the fragrance every few months.

Pretty lavender bags (made from old-fashioned lace or crisp gingham) look lovely in an airing cupboard and give a sweet fresh scent to your clothes and linens. Make sure you store clean bed-

winter scents

- Come winter, a lovely way to perfume a room is to drape garlands of scented pine cones over radiators to release their delicious scents.
- Tie your cones in a line with dark-colored cotton and then soak overnight in around 150ml (5fl oz) of water to which you have added 25–30 drops of essential oil.
- Cheering winter scents might include cedarwood, cinnamon, ginger, clove and geranium. Add a few bright ribbons and place on the radiator.
- You will need to resoak them every week or two if you want to keep the scent topped up.
- If you'd like something more subtle just pop a cotton wool ball or tissue scented with around six drops of oil behind a radiator.

THE SOUND FAST

If you're not sure how sound affects you, try living without it for a day or a weekend. Go on a sound fast – no television, no radio, no music, no inane chatter. If you share with people, see if you can manage a day in quiet companionship – if you need to say anything obviously you should, but try to cut out conversation for sound's sake. This can be a very interesting exercise. Many people find when they try it for the first time just how important silence and peace is to them. They also realize how much rubbish they speak just to be polite and sociable! Being silent can also be a real eye-opener on even deeper levels. When you stop the external chatter and noise, the mind can focus inwards and sometimes you can find quite unexpected insights appearing.

However, silence is not always golden: it can just be an interesting option to try from time to time. And, of course, there is never any such thing as real silence. Even if you live in the heart of the country, especially if you live in the heart of the country, there will be noises all around. The wind rustling the leaves in the trees; the crash of the ocean; the sound of rain falling on rooftops; the bark of a dog; the hum of a bee; the raucous din of the dawn chorus; the muffled silence that only a blanket of thick snow can bestow.

We should also investigate the healing power of sounds to see how they can help us create the haven we desire. Sound therapists have discovered that certain sounds have almost miraculous effects on both body and mind. French sound researcher Dr Alfred Tomatis believes that Gregorian chants and other sacred chants from around the world can help to harmonize the body, bringing peace, confidence – and even reducing the need for sleep. Other researchers have found that listening to certain kinds of music can calm and relax the entire body. There are 101 ways to introduce healing sounds into the home. The following are just a few ideas to get you started:

HEALING SOUNDS

Do you play an instrument? Does anyone else you know play? In the olden days, communal singing and dancing were wonderful ways of relaxing and winding down after work. Why not start your own singing circle? You don't have to be an expert; just enjoy the music. No instruments? Just use your voices: sing simple but spine-chillingly effective rounds.

Keep a wide repertoire of music to suit all your moods. Opera may be stirring and sophisticated but every so often almost everyone needs a dose of energizing rock or a sentimental blast of country music. Keep your musical tastes open.

Work out which music can put you into moods and get you out of them. You may only have to listen to a certain Rachmaninov concerto to be off, bawling your eyes out. A dash of Monteverdi may instantly put a smile on your face. Certain rock or pop tunes will always get your toes tapping; others will have you in floods of tears.

Imagine spending a day or even a weekend on a sound fast, when the only noise you hear from dawn until dusk is the sound of your own footsteps on a wooden floor.

Choose your music carefully when you have guests. Wagner is not great for the digestion, while an endless stream of reggae might give guests a thumping headache. Unless you know your guests share your taste in music go for a safe option: light classical music or mellow jazz are generally safe. Keep the volume low: the music should be providing a background, not competing with your conversation.

If you live in a very noisy neighborhood, invest in some recordings of soothing sounds from nature – and maybe a pair of earphones. The sound of birdsong, dolphins, whale music, waterfalls and the sea can give an instant sense of soothing peace. They can be useful if you're trying to meditate in a noisy place too.

Try singing or making sounds yourself. Most of us forget how to sing but it can be truly liberating. Sing along with the radio when you're on your own; sing old songs or make up your own; chant sacred sounds like 'omm' or vowel sounds like 'aah', 'eee' and 'ooo'. See how they affect you. Sing everywhere and anytime: in the garden or the bathroom; in the wind and rain; to the dawn and the dusk. Just sing.

simple sounds

- Search out simple sound-making equipment. Bells can be tinny and irritating or mellow and stunning. Find one whose voice suits you. Tibetan singing bowls make eerily mystical sounds. Drums echo our heartbeat – in Native American tradition you could make your own drum or buy one which 'calls' to you. Drumming can be very grounding and calming after a hard day's work.
- What did you play as a child? Get out your old recorder or xylophone. Make rattles out of washing-up liquid bottles filled with beans. Whittle a whistle from a piece of wood or bamboo.
- If you have had an argument and the room is feeling thick and unpleasant try breaking up the atmosphere with a party squeaker. The silly noise cuts through all the rotten feelings and brings a child-like innocence back into the room.
- Introduce natural sounds into your home: wind chimes, waterfalls and so on.

the feeling home

as you walk around your house are there things you just have to touch? The smooth-grained banister of old oak that curves around the staircase, or the rough texture of seagrass matting under your toes, perhaps? You may have a cosy blanket that you hunch into when it's cool and a polished piece of rose quartz that feels fresh on your forehead when the temperature soars. The feel and textures in your home are partly what gives an abode its 'feel-good factor'. By choosing fabrics and furnishings in a wide variety of textures you can do far more than

make your home look interesting and attractive. Every time your hands, feet, face (or indeed any part of you) come in touch with a different texture, it makes you focus on your body; it pulls you back out of your mind into a real sense of the here and now. It's like giving yourself a few moments of instant mindfulness meditation. All too often we drift through our days living in our heads and hearts, but rarely in our bodies. But a surprise to the senses can ground you like nothing else. A change in temperature from the warmth of a woollen carpet to the cool underfoot of stone; a shift from the smoothness of satin to the rough and readiness of hessian or jute gives you a nudge: you suddenly remember that you have a body once again.

Texture, as well as shape and design, can also make us feel comfortable or uncomfortable. 'Surfaces, textures and feel count for as much as efficiency,' Thomas Moore reminds us – and how right he is. So choose your textures with as much care for their feel as their washability; as much concern for the smile they bring to your face as their cost-effectiveness. Become aware of the rough and smooth; the cool and warm; the matt and the gloss; the etched and the furrowed.

Start by taking a look back to your answers to the 'touch' section on page 49. What are the literal 'feelings', the sensations you remembered when you thought about your most well-loved homes? If you're not sure or really don't feel very much in tune with this often forgotten sense of touch, then go on a texture-finding mission. Designers nowadays are realizing just how much fun they can have playing with different feels and textures on fabrics and furni-

ture so visit a few large stores and let your fingers do some exploring. As always, nature offers a whole store and more within a few paces of your front door – whether you live in the city or the country. Trees, stones, grass, leaves and plants: all have texture and a feel all of their own.

Like everything else in your home, the textures you choose are totally individual. There is no correct way of introducing texture, just whatever takes your mood and whatever makes your soul smile. But let's take a look at the enormous range of possibilities when it comes to texture and feel.

FABRICS

Feel the difference between silk and mohair; velvet and cashmere; linen and corduroy. Check out how pure wool feels next to a synthetic fiber; how a pure cotton garment varies from one mixed with acrylic. Don't just feel them with your fingers; run the fabric over your face, against your cheek. What does your skin tell you about this material? Each evokes a different mood, a new feeling, a totally fresh sensation.

COOL TEXTURES
If you put up crisp cotton curtains in a living room and cover your chairs with a nice slubbed-linen union, you will usher in a cool feel to the room.

Imagine the sheer sensual pleasure of waking up each morning and sinking your toes into the tufts of this long-haired rug.

TRIMMINGS

If you can't afford to buy new furniture or put up new drapes or soft furnishings, then go wild with some new trimmings. The finishing touches you add can totally change the appearance – and feel – of a room.

Plain cotton curtains could be invested with a deep fringe or an added border in a more tactile fabric. Tie-backs and tassels can transform curtains – they come in all kinds of fabrics, from chenille to silk, from wool to gold thread. Or you could make your own.

Ribbons, fringing and ropes can brighten up pillows and cushions and give new life to an old blind or bedspread. Beads give good feel-nice feelings too: you could make a fringe of them to edge a bedroom curtain or go totally wild and make a new curtain entirely out of beads (experiment with glass, ceramic and wooden beads to see which feels nicest as you push through its tendrils).

There are so many wonderful materials you can use in the home – once you free your imagination and let it wander. Basically, try to forget about the rules and let your senses take precedence over your brain. The end result may not be as practical as nylon, as hard-wearing as plastic and acrylic, but it will certainly feel a whole lot nicer. Before we end this chapter, here are just a few more idle thoughts on texture to tempt your senses into action.

TEXTURE TIPS

As the weather gets colder we crave cosy, warm, inviting textures. Maybe invest in a set of loose covers for your sofa or chairs in a rich inviting wool, velvet or moleskin. Or introduce a few throws and some more comforting pillows. Come summer it's all change again with crisp cottons and linens, cheery canvas and gingham.

Don't restrict yourself to the furnishing fabric department; look at dress fabrics too: they can make wonderful pillows, cushions and throws. Tweeds can give either a very modern or countrified air, depending on the colors and design you choose. But they are a little itchy so maybe stick to accessorizing with tweed rather than using it for covering chairs or sofas.

If you knit, make yourself some seriously desirable throws, blankets,

Most natural fabrics feel good just as they are, but for extra texture, why not consider adding a deep fringe to a favorite old tablecloth?

cushions and pillows in a variety of wools: from cool cottons to luxurious mohair and alpaca. Cable-knits in earthy homespun or creamy Aran give texture and cosiness combined: far too good to keep just for clothes.

Don't leave rugs and kilims just lying on the floors: they make hard-working, good-looking covers for sofas, chairs, footstools and cushions. They are also great at beating winter draughts – caught by clips onto a pole over a door, or rolled up into a solid draught-excluder.

Use pebbles and shells as interesting door knobs. Feel the difference between something smooth and round and something rough and gritty. Put different knobs on each door for a totally sense-expanding experience.

Collect some pieces of beautiful fine bone china – from junk shops or yard sales. Nothing matches the sensation on the lips of drinking from the finest porcelain. However ramshackle your surroundings, you can sit back with a cup of tea, close your eyes and imagine yourself taken back to a time of infinite refinement.

Think about using fabrics in unusual ways. If Ralph Lauren can take denim off jeans and put it on a sofa, why shouldn't you get inventive? Why should towelling just be for towels? Bright towels could make unusual blinds or mats for a bedroom. If you can't find the right color, they are easily dyed at home. A thick quilt could cover a draughty door, looking and feeling wonderful. Where is it written in stone that a tablecloth should always stay a tablecloth when it could make fabulous curtains?

Having used the tablecloth for curtains, lay your table with all manner of alternative 'tablecloths'. Make it irresistible to your guests so they can't help but stroke it! Sari fabric looks stunning for a party; soft velvet adds an air of decadent mystery. Or be really surrealistic and buy a length of fake fur or artificial grass!

Have 'touchy feely' bowls around your home. A bowl of sea-smoothed pebbles to feel between your fingers – or glossy shiny marbles, glinting glass. Fill a few bowls with different grades of sand – from the very finest to the quite rough. Clench your fists in the sand as you sit and relax or watch television: it feels great and can also help to release tension in your hands, wrists and fingers. If you have weak fingers it can strengthen them too. Other thoughts for bowls? Cool fresh moss perhaps? Or fill a glass container with colored water and colored oil. They should separate out to look jewel-like. If you plunge in your hand and move them together you should feel the coolness of the water mingling with the warmth of the oil. An instant hand-softener too.

the creative home

Objects are the symbols of the self. The things with which we surround ourselves are reflections of our inner being, markers of our soul. This was a lesson we learned back in Part One, but now it's time to pay some more attention to the bits and pieces which are scattered throughout our homes, and which say so much about us. Very few homes consist of just furniture and fabrics. Even the most minimalist of decorators usually places a few carefully chosen objects in equally carefully chosen spots. Look around your home and without doubt there will probably be hundreds of 'things' – pictures, paintings, ornaments, sculptures, knick-knacks and decorative items. Chosen carefully, they can make us smile when we're down; give us a sense of peace when we're feeling stressed; distract us when we're feeling out of sorts with the world. Bought without thought, placed without care, they can irritate or overwhelm us. Often they can make our homes seem homogenous, a series of Stepford homes without individuality, verve and soul.

There may be certain objects in your home which have no real purpose but which you simply love. A tiny Buddha placed on the desk top can provide a reminder that there is more to life than the daily grind and bring a little peace to every day. Pieces of hand-thrown pottery often have a rough, honest generosity which begs to be filled with food for friends or piles of nature's spoils. Items like these all lift the soul in some strange, unaccountable way.

THE POWER OF IMAGES

Images are powerful: they speak directly to the soul and can bring up intense, often forgotten emotions. If you find that hard to believe, see what happens if you pick up something connected with your childhood: an item similar to something you remember from your early home or maybe a modern replica of a favorite toy. Your hand curves around it; memories come flooding back; often you can be quite overwhelmed by the force of the past and the strength of your emotions.

Objects carry a definite charge – if they have a deep and meaningful resonance for us. Yet many of the things with which we fill our homes are somehow dead. They fill a gap; they provide a bit of color, maybe, but they do nothing for the soul. Why? Because it can be hard to feel love and affection, or even awe and respect, for mass-produced items, made by machines from synthetic materials which turn out all looking exactly the same as each other, as if off a conveyor belt. They may be fashionable, they might even have beautiful images, but there is often something strangely lifeless about them.

On the other hand, there is something alchemical about a craftsperson's act of creation. Something imagined by a human heart and lovingly brought into creation by a pair of human hands will have a magical, timeless quality – providing it has been made with true vision and care using natural materials or perhaps painted with evocations of nature or scored with beautiful inscriptions.

> *Beauty doesn't require prettiness. Some pieces of art are not pleasing to look at, and yet their content and form are arresting and lure the heart into profound imagination.*
>
> Thomas Moore, author of *Care of the Soul*

Above **The objects we choose to surround ourselves with contribute in a very real way to our feeling of wellbeing. They may not be very practical, but they speak to our souls.**

Right **A collection of items all the same type can make an interesting display. But before you begin, make sure you choose a theme that strikes a chord deep within you.**

PLANTS & FLOWERS

What easier and more delightful way is there to bring the spirit of the garden, of the wild, into your home than with a vase brimming with blooms or a radiantly healthy pot plant? Psychics say that each plant has its own attendant spirit: the logic-defying gardens at Findhorn in Scotland were supposedly cultivated by lovingly contacting these elemental spirits and asking for their aid. With this in mind, pay careful attention to the plants you invite into your house: make sure you feel a living bond with them. Discover their likes and dislikes: ferns will adore the steamy atmosphere of a bathroom; a cactus would loathe it, much preferring a hot, dry window ledge. An aspidistra or mother-in-law's tongue will put up with a darkish hall where a geranium would soon show its displeasure. In feng shui terms, plants with soft rounded leaves are good for chi; spiky plants are trickier and need plenty of room if they are not to cause disputes.

Flowers can instantly shift the mood of a room. Passionate reds, crimsons, purples and puce make for a spicy, exotic feel. Yellows and oranges are upbeat, friendly and cheering: how can you feel miserable with a sunflower smiling at you? Softer shades of blue, pink, mauve and white give a gentle, soft, healing energy.

GARDENING IDEAS

There are a million and one ways with plants and flowers – seek out your nearest bookshop for literally hundreds of books. In the meantime, try these ideas for inspiration:

Plant bulbs for every season: you can't match the wonder of a bulb pushing through the soil, and they make startling conversation pieces. Of course, there are the usual favorites, such as daffodils, tulips and hyacinths, but try also exotic lilies and amaryllis.

Flowers do not have to mean expensive florist's blooms: think about jugs full of blossom; branches with sticky buds in spring; armfuls of greenery. Pick bunches of herbs for sweet-smelling displays which will also help keep the bugs at bay.

Plant window boxes for a year-round display of color and scent. Choose sweet-smelling and night-flowering plants for your bedroom window: night-scented stocks, tobacco plants and lavender.

Plunder the vegetable garden for unusual feature plants: onions, garlic and especially leeks make the most architectural buds and then explode in a crazy globular head of white or pink. Transplant into an indoor pot, watch and wonder.

Make your own topiary: with box if you have the patience of a saint or, if you would like a speedier result, make or buy a wire frame and train obliging ivy into pompoms, standards, even rabbits or teddy bears.

Leave small posies of flowers in unexpected places for your guests. A few sprigs of lavender tied with ribbon on the pillow pinned to a note saying 'sweet dreams'; a circle of daisies around the saucer for an early morning cup of tea; rose petals sprinkled amidst the towels; herb twigs under the soap dish; bright gerberas around the base of a candle; edible flowers (borage, nasturtium, elderflower, woodruff, chive flowers, etc.) on cakes, amongst a plate of cookies, in punches – but do make sure you have not brought in the bugs too.

Grow cress as you did when you were a child: trace out your initials on damp blotting paper then add the seeds; or for a more dramatic effect dye the blotting paper and then sow your seeds into attractive symbols or patterns. If you get carried away you could make a living 'door mat' by sowing grass or chamomile seed on a natural coir or jute mat sprinkled with earth and keeping it damp.

Flowers can create different moods and feelings within us. White tulips have a cool, clinical charm and a feeling of serenity, while a jug of brightly colored sunflowers will lift the spirits and cheer up any room with their earthy boldness.

a space of your own

A QUIET CORNER

Perhaps you don't have the luxury of a whole room to yourself. It doesn't matter – you can still find a place for the soul in the smallest space, in the busiest, most totally shared home. You just have to think in a more interior way – and be rather more inventive.

In Russian orthodox spirituality there is a concept known as 'poustina'. Poustina can mean either a physical place, a retreat, or the secret place inside you – the hermitage within. It's a lovely thought: that even in the busiest, most crowded place, no-one can enter into our own internal poustina – unless we invite them. This sense of creating an internal sanctuary is how people have survived against incredible odds and is something worth remembering if, by now, you are moaning that you cannot possibly create a sanctuary – because you simply don't have the space.

In actual fact few of us are so impoverished of space that we cannot find a single corner to call our own. Think laterally. Are there any spaces in your home which are neglected or not used? Do you have a dusty attic which could be transformed into a private retreat? Or a cellar or shed? Could you colonize the greenhouse or clear out the 'junk' room? If not, start to think about the places in the home in which you feel most comfortable and secure. 'Most of us have a

Even the most unprepossessing corner can be transformed into a healing sanctuary if you are determined to make it work.

favorite chair or seat' says David Pearson, author of *The Natural House Book*, 'the old inglenook within a large fireplace and the rocking chair by the kitchen range…a half-hidden window seat, secluded corners, nooks and crannies, the seat on a verandah…'

Of course, he's right but some of us don't have quite such romantic spots in our homes. But other places can be just as soothing: a particular step on the stairs; the kitchen table when everyone has gone; a rug in front of the fire; the bathroom or laundry room. Perhaps there is a quiet corner somewhere? Might you perhaps create your own private space with the help of a screen or curtain?

Once again, it often seems that women lose out in this area. It's a common tradition (still) for a particular chair to be designated 'Father's chair', and a man can often still retreat to a study or a den. But women rarely have their own spaces – or even their 'own' pieces of furniture. Hestia, and a woman's inner need for calm reflection, is hurt by this lack. So too is that other archetypal goddess, Artemis, the virginal huntress who craves solitude and peace – away from the needs and demands of people. Even Athena, the goddess of wisdom, appreciates a place of her own – somewhere to read and study and flex her mind. Remember, too, that Athena was also a weaver – and activities such as weaving, knitting and needlepoint are perfect forms of meditation in which one is soothed by the rhythm of the loom or the needle into a place of quiet musing or even no thought. So, for the sake of your soul, reclaim a chair, or a corner – just somewhere which has your name stamped on it; where others knock before entering or ask before using.

Above all, remember that concept of poustina. If you are feeling harried and that you will never manage to carve out even the tiniest physical place for your soul, remind yourself that your sacred space can be one which relies more on time than physical place. If you set aside an hour or so a day just for you and your soul work, the physical location can easily shift according to circumstances. If the children are at school, take over the playroom. If your partner is at work, use the bedroom. But for that time, make sure it is all yours – a place out of time. Take a tip from hotels: make yourself a good old-fashioned sign which says 'DO NOT DISTURB', or words to that effect. Gently but firmly tell your family, room-mates, friends, neighbors and so on that there are some times when you have to be by yourself to give your soul some peace.

The awkward space under the stairs is often turned into a place for a desk or a home office, but why not screen it off and make it your sanctuary?

creating an altar

another way to invite a sense of sanctuary into your home involves even less space. You can simply set up an altar or a series of altars around your house. The word altar tends to conjure up images of High Church or pagan rituals but an altar is simply a place of spiritual focus, a small hearth for the spirit. Humans have always built altars or shrines, it seems. Evidence from Neolithic times shows our ancient ancestors kept certain places sacred and invested them with a numinous quality. In ancient Greece and Rome, as we have already seen, altars

were built within every house for the lares and penates, and other gods. But nowadays few Western homes (apart from those belonging to people with an orthodox faith) have any vestige of sacred places or shrines. And yet an altar is a simple thing to erect. All it takes is a small space – it could be a window ledge, a table top, part of your desk, a bookshelf…It's more than likely that the moment you read those words you will automatically know the spot or spots. Possibly, in a small or totally unconscious way, you have already made some kind of altar there. Maybe it's a couple of beloved photographs. Perhaps a crystal or a candle. You might have an incense burner and have positioned a vase of flowers next to it.

These are altars in themselves – small places of focus which make you want to stop, pause, ponder, say a prayer maybe or remember someone with love. What you put on your altar is totally up to you. But they should be things that speak directly to your soul. Not 'look-good' things; not even particularly 'feel-good' things but things that have a deep resonance for you.

Sometimes the items on an altar can be very soothing, but more often they will trigger all manner of emotions: tapping into your soul lessons. They might even make you recall and ponder your fears, your insecurities,

An altar need not be quite as grand as it sounds – in fact, it may be that you have unconsciously created altars all over your house already. All it requires are a few items that are of special significance to you.

your needs. The Hindu goddess Kali is a good case in point. Kali is a powerful goddess of life and strength but she is also the devourer who dances on the bodies of the dead with a necklace of skulls hung around her neck. Yet the lesson of Kali is deep and important: there is no life without death; no growth without decay; nothing new without the departure of the old. So choose your altar items with care and change them as and when you feel the need.

AN ALTAR OF THE ELEMENTS

If you are not sure what to put on your altar then follow the old, tried and tested formulae. In most traditional cultures, an altar is built using things that represent the four elements. So earth is honored with something living, such as a plant, or with the fabric of the earth – a stone, a bowl of earth, maybe a ceramic pot or a beautiful piece of wood. Air is traditionally represented by incense as the smoke moves through the air toward heaven – you can easily buy incense sticks or freshly made incense which you burn using a charcoal block on a fire-proof container. If you're not keen on incense you could substitute an aromatherapy oil burner with the same effect. Fire is obviously represented by candles. Water can easily be evoked with a bowl of clear, fresh water or something brought from the sea or river – some sand or a pebble or shell. In addition, you could add a favorite image – maybe a mandala, a goddess, saint or angel; perhaps a statue, a crystal, some fresh flowers... Most people, even those who work in the busiest offices, tend to 'decorate' their computers. If your workplace is the kitchen, you may find you have done something similar with your fridge or window ledge. We can't help it – deep within our souls is the need for these simple shrines.

SPIRITUAL PROTECTION

Why stop at your computer or the fridge door? In early times it was common to see signs of protection and prayer all around the house: the threshold was often protected against evil by burying a knife, crossed scissors or something iron beneath it. Horseshoes hung over the door to the house and the barn as a symbol of good luck and to keep the Devil away. In the Greek Islands garlands of garlic and wild flowers are commonly hung on village doors – they say it is to keep away the vampires and evil spirits. In the UK the same was done with wreaths of flowers at May Day and Yule. In India

you will often see doors and even their hinges painted with protective patterns. In traditional societies all over the world buildings were painted with symbols to keep away evil. Windows had particular safe-keeping designs, and glass balls and mirrors were hung in windows to ward off bad spirits.

A portrait of a much-loved person, surrounded by a few of his most precious possessions, is a good way to create an altar dedicated to the memory of a dead relative or friend. Light the candles when you come to stand or sit before it.

Although we are not so superstitious nowadays (or like to think we're not) there is something delightful about giving spiritual protection to your house in the age-old ways. Why not try bringing back the witch balls and protective horseshoes, or painting symbols and patterns on doors and window shutters? They look charming and make your home your own. They also honor the spiritual life of the soul and serve to invest seemingly inanimate objects or things with spirit.

MORE WATERY MAGIC

There are plenty of other ways to luxuriate in the the element of water. Here are a few ideas for immersing yourself in some watery magic:

Go for a bout of outdoor bathing – not just a quick dip in a pool but maybe an invigorating shower under a waterfall or a contemplative float on a pond or lake. Some adventurous souls have even rigged up showers and baths in their back yards – or out in the fields. You can buy solar-heated outdoor showers from camping shops. Just imagine bathing surrounded by a field of daisies or looking up at trees or even stars.

Try out communal bathing for a link back to the former great age of bathing. Seek out local steam baths; laze in a sauna; take the 'waters' if you have the luck to live near a healing spa or hot springs. Try to enjoy all kinds of curious bathing experiences – from a hot tub under the stars in Grand Bahama to a sulphurous hellfire pool in Wyoming to a clear mountain pool in Wales. If you're on holiday, find out the how the locals bathe and see if you can join in.

bathroom makeover

Give your bathroom a makeover. It needn't cost a fortune.

- Tiles can be painted over – ask at a specialist paint shop. So can that ghastly vinyl wallpaper you often get in bathrooms.
- Strip away nasty old carpet or synthetic flooring and either polish or paint the bare boards if they're in good condition. If not, check out the lovely pure-cotton floor coverings that are now available – or buy a deliciously patterned rug.
- Clear away all the clutter.
- Cover eye-sores with some generous drapes of fabric.
- Put up some pictures – or paint your own frescoes in pure Roman spa style.

If you're lucky enough to have a hot tub, indulge. An outdoor open tub? What complete bliss. If you don't have one, make it a good reason to visit a spa. While you're there explore all the other kinds of bath therapy: steams, saunas, water aerobics, watsu (shiatsu in the water). If you can find a naturopathic spa you can discover the joys of hydrotherapy – some are delicious, some are sheer torture!

Although very few of us are lucky enough to have access to an indoor swimming pool with a view of the sky like this one, a spot of moonlight bathing, gazing at the stars while you swim, is a delicious occupation that everyone should experience at least once.

Investigate the healing powers of mud. Certain mud is said to contain thousands of minerals and herbs that the body can take up and use. Visit your local health shop and see what's on offer – it's very messy but totally relaxing.

While you're soaking either drift and dream or flex your powers of imagination. Visualize yourself soaking in a clear mountain pool, or the warm gentle ocean. You are feeling warm and calm and deeply relaxed. Take the opportunity to give yourself some generous self-talk. Tell yourself you're great; you're feeling and looking good; you love and appreciate your body, whatever its shape.

Imagine beautiful nymphs, the handmaidens of Aphrodite, coming down to help you with your bath – they might wash your hair or manicure your nails, or simply tell you how wonderful you are. They could give you gifts: more self-esteem, a huge dose of confidence, a better body image, laughter, joy, a few moments of peace and quiet…

Turn simple routines such as bathing, cleansing your face and washing your teeth into rituals by being mindful. Be aware as you perform each task. Do it carefully, thoughtfully. Think about the day to come or the day that has just gone. Ponder on the things you hope to achieve or the good things that have happened. Use it as a small piece of quiet, alone time – to prepare, to reflect, to be with yourself.

Two books are highly recommend for your bathroom shelf. Michelle Dominique Leigh's book, *The New Beauty*, gives not just practical recipes and ideas for beauty and bathing, but also thought and meditations that allow you to follow the 'Zen' of bathing. Another favorite, which gives baths for virtually every occasion and mood, is *Water Magic* by Mary Muryn (see Bibliography for full details). It might be worth covering them in some protective plastic!

the
helping
home

love and romance

W hen you live in a clean, uncluttered home your mind should be free and clear. When your place is filled with inspiring colors and beautiful objects of the soul, life should start to move more easily and effortlessly. Yet sometimes, despite all your best efforts, that just doesn't happen. You might still feel stuck, caught tight in the middle of problems, frustrated and depressed. Of course a house can't fix everything in your life (sometimes you have to look for answers outside your four walls) but it can often give a helping hand. By using

techniques from feng shui and other forms of house-healing, it might even help you solve your problems – in the most surprising and unexpected ways. In the next couple of sections we're going to look at some surprisingly simple tips that might just help some of life's most common dilemmas. Let's start with the one that is probably the most important – and the one which usually causes the most problems – relationships.

LOVE AND RELATIONSHIPS

Whether you want a new relationship or would like to improve an existing one, feng shui has some straightforward tips to offer.

Presumably you will have already checked the marriage area of the home and, if it is missing or truncated, have taken steps to pull it back into the house. If possible, you should also have moved your bedroom to the marriage area or put your bed in the marriage corner of your bedroom. If you haven't done so yet, check out the initial guidelines for feng shui in Part Four. Having sorted out the basics, here are some more things you can do:

FENG SHUI FOR RELATIONSHIPS

Boost your marriage area by placing a beautiful bright light in the corner – a glittering chandelier is ideal (providing it suits your house) or check out stunning modern lights. A large lamp would work too, with a vibrant (ideally red or pink) lampshade. Add a vase full of gorgeous sensual flowers in romantic shades of red and pink.

Check again to make sure you are not filling your bedroom with things that represent your work – or a past relationship. If your bedroom is dedicated to the past or your career, it will leave you wedded to your work or a past love. Keep your bedroom just for sleep. If you have to work in your room, screen your work corner off and switch off the phone at night.

The images with which you surround yourself are very important. If the pictures around you are of solitary people or lonely landscapes (however beautiful they may be) you are symbolically cutting yourself off from relationships. In your bedroom it is essential you choose pictures of couples or soft, romantic landscapes.

Choose soft materials and gentle, rounded shapes for your bedroom. Curved lines usher in feelings of harmony and love. Your bedroom should be a sensual retreat so choose furniture, coverings and, particularly, your bed, for comfort above all else. Fabrics should be sensuous and feel good against the skin; pile your bed with sumptuous cushions and pillows for lounging.

Candles represent the element of fire and also symbolize passion. Choose red candles if you're looking for a wild love life; pink for romance – or, even better, have a collection of various pinks and reds for the full range of emotions. Their light is soft and soothing – and may get your love life glowing.

Place a beautiful light in the corner of your marriage area and use lots of pink, the color of romance, to give your relationship a loving boost.

HELP FOR SPECIFIC PROBLEMS

If you have a particular difficulty in your love life, try these tips.

ATTRACTING A NEW PARTNER

In her book, *Interior Design with Feng Shui*, Sarah Rossbach relates a 'cure' for people who want to get married – but it would work simply for a new relationship as well. She points out that if you're already in a relationship and want it to stay happy and contented you can follow the same advice. You need to obtain nine objects from a newly married couple or have the couple touch nine of your own objects, either on their wedding day itself, or within 90 days of the wedding. Then visualize yourself acquiring the bride's marriage chi as she hands over the objects. Put the objects in the marriage position of your bedroom.

Many people find it hard to attract a new relationship because they are not sure what they truly want – or feel worried they will repeat past mistakes, or are simply scared of the commitment of a relationship. If you feel your past is preventing you from finding love, it could be worthwhile talking over your fears with a therapist or counselor. Often a fresh perspective can totally change the situation.

You can also adapt the exercises given earlier in this book to discover what you truly want and need from a partner. Think about past relationships (what you liked; what you didn't like; what patterns repeated themselves). Try the Miracle Question technique (see Part Two), thinking how you would be and feel and act if you met your ideal partner.

Put together a 'love map' (just as you did with the treasure map in Part Two) and hang it in your marriage corner. Ask your house for guidance. What is holding you back from having a relationship?

REKINDLING A ROCKY RELATIONSHIP

Check your home and particularly your marriage area for things that may be quite literally unstable. This could be a precarious three-legged table or some overly delicate vases or ornaments which could break if you even looked at them. Try to make sure your house is filled with unequivocal, solid, permanent, earthed things which cannot budge or be shifted.

You need to weigh your relationship, and your marriage area in particular, down so put something very stable in the marriage corner of your house – maybe a good solid four-legged table or a big plump sofa (something that is well rooted to the ground and doesn't wobble). Add something hearty like a big earthenware pot or a solid statue or stone to the marriage corner of your bedroom (if your bed isn't already there).

Check the fabrics in your bedroom – are they flimsy, delicate and floaty? Replace them with something more robust. Perhaps some luscious thick velvet curtains or a beautiful warm woollen blanket tucked in tight; or a weighty quilt or comforter.

Check there aren't too many doors in your bedroom or marriage area – if there are, maybe cover one or two over with a rich thick curtain or tapestry.

A volatile relationship can be calmed down by making sure that all the imagery in your bedroom depicts loving couples or romantic scenes of 'letting go' – stormy seas or dramatic landscapes will only serve to stir up even more trouble.

Look at your desk as well. Make sure there is nothing flimsy which can be blown away on it. As with the house, your marriage area is in the far right-hand corner – put something good and solid there, maybe a photo of the two of you in a thick heavy frame. Weigh it down even more with a solid red pot with a healthy plant or a big beautiful stone.

CALMING A VOLATILE RELATIONSHIP

If you're always fighting and would like a little peace and quiet in your relationship, start by choosing soothing colors in your marriage area and (if it's different) your bedroom. Although feng shui usually recommends warm pinks and soft reds for bedrooms, if a relationship is too sparky try soothing blues and greens to settle the energy.

Pictures again are important so take down the dramatic landscapes or the photos of flamenco dancers and passionate lovers and choose something which is more light-hearted and fun: photos of children playing innocently can be very calming. Feng shui experts also recommend images of letting-go – pictures of birds being released, of balloons taking off, of boats launching from a dock.

ENTICING PASSION INTO YOUR LIFE

Fire is the element that governs passion so stock up on candles, particularly in spicy tones of red or bright pink. You don't need to surround yourself with images from the *Kama Sutra* or buy erotic prints – but do pick paintings or posters that use passionate colors and a passionate technique. Abstracts can be full of life, vigor and passion.

Hot up the colors in your bedroom using passionate reds – not necessarily all over but as accent colors.

And anything flame-shaped is good too – an exception to the feng shui rule of soft shapes. Think about triangular or diamond-shaped cushions maybe, or put a throw folded or diagonally across your bed so it makes a triangle or diamond.

TO SAVE A RELATIONSHIP

If you really feel your relationship is on the rocks, if you are on the verge of separation or even divorce, you need to step back, gain some objectivity and look at the whole situation without being drawn into recriminations and anger. You are looking for clarity in your life so start by cleaning once again. Above all, clean the windows (the eyes of the house) so you can see with pure vision. Get rid of the cobwebs, make sure your lights are gleaming and that there are no broken light bulbs.

Keep your bedroom brightly and clearly lit – avoid shadows and half-light that may disguise your real feelings.

Try the Miracle Question technique again: how would you know if your problem had been solved; what would be different; how would you act; how would your partner act; how would your friends and family act? What would it take for a reconciliation?

career, creativity & money

by following simple feng shui guidelines you can also help to boost your career, your creativity and even bring more money into your life. Before carrying out any of these tips, check the earlier sections on cleaning, clearing and feng shui to make sure you have the ground rules in place. Often all you need to get the dice rolling is to do a serious bout of spring cleaning, clutter-clearing and some basic feng shui. If the problem still remains once you've done all that, try these hints.

BOOSTING YOUR CAREER

For most people, their career area will be surrounding the front door, or directly to the right or left of it. If your front door lies in the career area then make sure it is as clean and smoothly working as possible. It should open easily (if it sticks, get it fixed at once). It should be freshly painted or polished, with any door furniture (knobs, letter-boxes, key holes etc.) absolutely gleaming. No cobwebs, no dirty marks, no peeling paint. Wind chimes which tinkle as you enter are great for energizing this area.

If you want to stabilize your career then make sure you have a good solid pot or statue either side of the door (either on the outside or inside of the door).

Feng shui expert William Spear points out that the Chinese connect the career area with water (which is also linked with money and wealth) so he suggests you boost this area with objects that contain liquid such as inks, paint, medicine or oils. Maybe an oil burner with jewel-like colored oils, or a beautiful bowl containing water on which you could float candles or flower petals. Pictures and photographs in this spot should depict water in some way: so look out for images which include rivers, streams, oceans, fish, whales, waterfalls etc.

Your desk is also symbolic of your career so pay attention to it. If you work in commerce and deal with money you should choose a square or rectangular desk. If creativity is your priority, then an oval or round desk is better. If you want both, choose a desk that com-bines graceful lines with defined, square edges. Natural wood is the best choice – black and white desks will tend to slow you down. Make sure there is nothing hanging above the desk – no plants, mobiles or light fixtures.

In an ideal world the desk would be in a diagonal position to the door of your office so you had a clear view of the door. If you can't move your desk and have your back to the door, you must have a mirror on your desk to give you a view of the door. That alone might save your career!

Get rid of all the clutter and put your files and papers in neat order. If you feel you always have too much work, get rid of the stacks of dealt-with papers – file them out of sight in a vertical drawer filing unit.

Now look at your clear desk and add objects to boost the ba-gua of your desk space. Put a vase of flowers, a plant or a beautiful crystal in the top left-hand corner. A picture of your family or partner is good for the top right-hand corner; or an image of unity, warmth and love. This will help humanize your working life and make it more harmonious. On your right-hand side is 'helpful people', so it's a natural place for the phone (if you're right-handed); also for your address book (put a lead crystal on top to boost it). If you're left-handed your phone can sit in 'knowledge' very happily. If not, keep your reference books there. Straight in front of you – at the far end of the desk or on your computer, is your fame area. This is a good place to keep something that inspires your soul – a picture, a statue, a candle.

ATTRACTING WEALTH

If you have cleared and decluttered your wealth area and 'cured' any missing bits, and you're still having trouble paying the bills, let's take a look at what else you could do:

- Check your front and back doors – if they lie in a straight line, this could be your problem. Place a plant in between the two doors or hang a small spherical crystal below the level of the doors, making the chi energy pause. Are your doors too big in proportion to the size of your house or office? That too could cause money to disperse. Place a good, heavy, solid object at the entrance, near the door – or invest in a pair of large stone urns to steady the energy either side of the door.
- Goldfish are a well-known Chinese way of enticing wealth into your home. Put your bowl or tank in the wealth area of your home or your study/office. For best results you should have nine fish – eight red and one black. Make sure your tank is kept clean and that your fish have enough space. An aerator helps keep the tank oxygenated and boosts chi too. If you're not happy with the idea of keeping fish, just install a waterfall or small fountain to pump water around.
- Red and green are the colors traditionally associated with wealth. It is not necessary to decorate in these colors (unless you happen to like the combination) but just make sure you have something in these colors in your wealth area. A healthy green plant could help – put it in a bright-red pot for maximum effectiveness.
- If you find it easy enough to get hold of money but that it then simply vanishes before your very eyes, you need to weigh down your wealth area. Try putting something solid – a heavy stone, plant, statue or piece of furniture – in that corner.
- Make sure your wealth corner gets plenty of bright light. If it's naturally dark, place a large lamp there to give it some illumination.
- Check your kitchen. Remember that kitchens are also equated with wealth in feng shui terms. So ensure it's bright and well-lit and free from all clutter. Your stove in particular must be kept clean and well-working at all times. If the burners are clogged you will never clear your debts. Use all the burners, not just the front ones – the more burners used, the more money earned.
- Check your bathroom too. Keep the toilet seat always down or you're flushing money away.

If you're lucky enough to have a swimming pool, you shouldn't have too many problems with wealth (bit of a swings and roundabout this one: if you've got a swimming pool you're probably wealthy in the first place!). However, they can be a bit tricky. A swimming pool inside the house can unbalance it – unless your house is truly huge it's not a good idea. Circular-shaped pools are best and the pool should not be sited too close to the house or it will overwhelm it. If so, put a curving path of rounded stepping stones between pool and house. If a swimming pool is out of your price range, then a garden pond can be equally effective. Again it should be rounded, away from the house and kept clean.

The size and shape of your desk, its postition in the room and how you arrange things on it can have an enormous influence on how your career progresses. This tidy desk sits diagonally in front of the door – an ideal position in feng shui terms.

ENHANCING CREATIVITY

Have you always wanted to write a book? Or paint or ice cakes? Or start an innovative business? If so, focus on your study or the room in which you do your creative work. Try these tips and see if they help:

Put up a wind chime by the door so it tinkles as you walk in. This will clear the energy of the room and also signify to your subconscious that you are entering a different place and will focus you on your work.

Directly in front of you (on your desk or worktable) put something that links you to your dreams, something that makes you focus on what you want to achieve. It could be a picture, the cover of a book, anything that symbolizes your dreams or projects. If you have a computer taking up that space, put it on the wall beyond. Feng shui consultant Sarah Shurety tells the tale of a woman who wanted to set up a refuge for animals and so she made a collage and put up pictures of animals plus the business cards of various firms she was hoping would sponsor her project. The refuge became a huge success.

Once again, water can help. Sarah recommends having a small fountain in your office because the bubbling water helps creativity (as well as attracting money – no bad combination). It will also bring in clarity and lessen stress. Ideally place it near the entrance of your study or in the wealth area.

Make sure you have a bright light in the left-hand corner of your work table or desk. An uplighter is ideal.

Always keep fresh flowers on your desk to inspire you, or a healthy, green-leaved plant.

The ideal place for books is in the knowledge area of your office or your desk. Never pack a bookcase so tightly that there is no room for any more books. Symbolically this means that there is no space for new knowledge or inspiration in your life, so leave a few gaps in your shelves.

You could also use the treasure map technique again – focusing on your goals and aims. Place the map you have made in front of you so you can see it as you work.

Burn uplifting, inspiring oils as you work. The scents will help clear your head and focus your attention, but also turn the place where you work into an oasis of calm and tranquillity – see Part Five for ideas on the best oils to use for your purpose.

Windchimes are an excellent feng shui cure that is useful in all sorts of different situations. They are particularly good at stirring up chi in a place that has stagnant energy, but make sure you hang them in a place where the breeze has a chance to stir them.

the journey ends – and begins

We've been on a long and intriguing journey through the home. It is hoped that, by now, you feel closer to your home; that it has become, not just a practical place in which to eat and sleep, but also something closer to a healing sanctuary. It may even feel like a warm and loving friend. Just as a good friend will provide a shoulder to cry on, good advice and a warm pair of comforting arms, so your home can embrace you and give you comfort, whenever you need it.

Throughout this book there is plenty of good, solid, practical advice on how to transform the space you live in. But do remember that, as important as feng shui and space cleansing and decluttering are, the most crucial part of the whole process is you. Your intuition, your imagination, your intent. The process of turning a building into a home doesn't take money and you don't need a degree in interior design; but it does take heart and you do need soul.

By now you will probably have realized that putting the soul into a home is pretty much the same process as finding your own soul, your true inner Self. For you cannot truly achieve one without discovering something about the other. Becoming aware of the world of spirit all around us; tuning in to your own intuitive powers; becoming sensitive to your senses and how they react to light, color, sound, scent, touch and taste – these are all a part of discovering the loves and boundaries of your own soul.

Meeting and living with the deep archetypes which dwell in the house of the spirit – Hestia, Aphrodite, Artemis, Hermes and their companions – opens the soul to its very depths.

Discovering that everything, be it a fire or a table, a vase or a wastepaper bin, has its own subtle energy can change the entire way we view the world – and our position in it. We can begin to understand that we are all truly a part of the world – and the world is within us as well as without. We are all vital parts of the rhythm of life, the dance of nature on this planet. That knowledge can bring us beyond the boundaries of our own four walls into a deeper sense of belonging on the Earth itself, our larger home.

There is only so much a book like this can do. And there is only so much a book like this needs to do. Now you have the tools, it's up to you to use them as you feel is right. If you have not yet found the time to go through the exercises in Part Two, why not have a go. Once you feel comfortable with the techniques (and they really are very simple) you can use them for accessing a power beyond your rational, conscious mind. They can all easily be adapted to help you find answers to most problems and difficulties in life.

If you just allow yourself to be calm and quiet, to go into a state of deep relaxation, you may well find the answers you need. If you have a tough decision to make, why not ask your home for some help? If you need to find more time for yourself, call on Hestia's quiet wisdom. If you need some clever answers to tricky problems, try asking Hermes for some bright ideas. If you're feeling vulnerable and downhearted, ask the guardian angels of the home to enfold you in their strong and loving wings. You are never alone when you become aware of the spirit of your home.

It's up to you to use your imagination and intuition to create a space that is unique and personal to you: not just a home but a true sanctuary.

Of course you might ask whether you are really talking to your house or these gods? Or are you simply accessing your higher Self or your unconscious mind? Surely it doesn't really matter. What counts is that, by stilling the restless, panicking, conscious mind, you can allow some answers to come from a quieter, calmer, wiser

place. It is a very pleasant notion to think our homes could be directly helping us, especially if you have a rather romantic streak. But rest assured that, if you ask, you will be answered. Providing you can find the time to stop and quietly listen.

If this book has one purpose, it is to request that you do find the time – for your soul's sake. If you give yourself nothing else in life, give yourself the gift of time. Not hours and hours of it, but the odd quiet half hour or hour – just for you. Find that favorite spot in the house, be it a comfy armchair or an odd corner, and give yourself time to simply be. Allow the peace to fall upon you and let your mind drift off and away. Give your home and your soul the chance to work together in a silent healing.

bibliography

Ban Breathnach, Sarah. *Simple Abundance*, Warner Books, New York, 1995

Bloom, William. *Psychic Protection*, Piatkus, London, 1996

Bridges, Carol. *A Soul in Place*, Earth Nation Publishing, Nashville, 1995

Brown, Simon. *The Principles of Feng Shui*, Thorsons, London, 1996

Buchman, Dian Dincin. *The Complete Book of Water Therapy*, Keats, New Canaan, 1994

Budapest, Zsuzsanna E. *The Goddess in the Bedroom*, HarperCollins, New York, 1995

Chaitow, Leon. *Body Tonic*, Gaia, London, 1995

Chiazzari, Suzy. *The Healing Home*, Ebury Press, London, 1997

Chuen, Master Lam Kam. *The Feng Shui Handbook*, Gaia, London, 1995

Clarke, David with Roberts, Andy. *Twilight of the Celtic Gods*, Blandford, London, 1996

Cooper, David. *Silence, Simplicity and Solitude*, Bell Tower, New York, 1992

Day, Christopher. *Places of the Soul*, Thorsons, London, 1990

Demetrakopoulos, Stephanie A. 'Hestia, Goddess of the Hearth', in Spring 1979, Spring Publications, Irving, 1979

Dewhurst-Maddock, Olivea. *Healing with Sound*, Gaia, London, 1993

Downing, Damien. *Day Light Robbery*, Arrow, London, 1988

Dowrick, Stephanie. *The Intimacy & Solitude Self-Therapy Book*, Women's Press, London, 1993

Fairchild, Dennis. *Healing Homes*, WaveField Books, Birmingham MI, 1996

Fox, Matthew & Sheldrake, Rupert. *The Physics of Angels*, HarperCollins, New York, 1996

Gimbel, Theo. *The Book of Colour Healing*, Gaia, London, 1994

Goldman, Jonathan. *Healing Sounds*, Element, Shaftesbury, 1992

Hillman, James (ed.). *Facing the Gods*, Spring, Dallas, 1980

Holbeche, Soozi. *The Power of Gems and Crystals*, Piatkus, London, 1989

Johnson, Robert A. *Owning Your Own Shadow*, HarperSanFrancisco, New York, 1991

Jordan, Michael. *The Encyclopedia of Gods*, Kyle Cathie, London, 1992

Jung, C G. *Memories, Dreams, Reflections*, Pantheon, New York, 1961

Kabat-Zinn, Jon. *Mindfulness Meditation for Everyday Life*, Piatkus, London, 1994

Kingston, Karen. *Creating Sacred Space with Feng Shui*, Piatkus, London, 1996

Lacy, Marie Louise. *The Power of Colour to Heal the Environment*, Rainbow Bridge Publications, London, 1996

Larousse. *Dictionary of World Folklore*, Larousse, Edinburgh, 1995

Leigh, Michelle Dominique. *The New Beauty*, Newleaf, London, 1996

Liberman, Jacob. *Light – Medicine of the Future*, Bear & Company, Sante Fe, 1991

Linn, Denise. *Sacred Space*, Rider, London, 1995

Lawlor, Anthony. *The Temple in the House*, Tarcher/Putnam, New York, 1994

Logan, Karen. *Clean House, Clean Planet*, Pocket Books, New York, 1993

MacDonald Baker, Sidney. *Detoxification & Healing*, Keats, New Canaan, 1997

Marc, Olivier. *Psychology of the House*, Thames & Hudson, London, 1977

Marcus, Clare Cooper. *House as a Mirror of Self*, Conari Press, Berkeley, 1995

McIntyre, Anne. *The Complete Floral Healer*, Gaia, London, 1996

Mella, Dorothee L. *The Language of Colour*, Michael Joseph, London, 1988

Ming-Dao, Deng. *Everyday Tao*, HarperCollins, New York, 1996

Mitchell, Jann. *Home Sweeter Home*, Hillsboro, 1996

Mojay, Gabriel. *Aromatherapy for Healing the Spirit*, Gaia, London, 1996

Moran, Victoria. *Shelter for the Spirit*, HarperCollins, New York, 1997

Moore, Thomas. *Care of the Soul*, HarperCollins, New York, 1992

Moore, Thomas (ed.). *The Essential James Hillman*, Routledge, London, 1990

Muryn, Mary. *Water Magic*, Bantam, London, 1997

Nahmad, Claire. *Earth Magic*, Rider, London, 1993

Null, Gary. *The Healthy Body Book*, Health Communications, Deerfield Beach, 1994

Pagram, Beverly. *Natural Housekeeping*, Gaia, London, 1997

Palmer, Magda. *The Healing Power of Crystals*, Rider, London, 1988

Palmer, Martin & Nigel. *Sacred Britain*, Piatkus, London, 1997

Paris, Ginette. *Pagan Meditations – Aphrodite, Hestia, Artemis*, Spring, Woodstock, 1986

Paungger, Johanna & Poppe, Thomas. *Moon Time*, CW Daniel, Saffron Walden, 1995

Pearson, David. *The Natural House Book*, Gaia, London, 1989

Pearson, David. *The Natural House Catalog*, Gaia, London, 1996

Petersen, Brenda. *Nature and Other Mothers*, HarperCollins, New York, 1992

Rinpoch, Sogyal. *The Tibetan Book of Living and Dying*, Rider, London, 1992

Rossbach, Sarah & Yun, Lin. *Living Color*, Kodansha International, New York, 1994.

Rossbach, Sarah. *Feng Shui*, Rider, London, 1984

Rossbach, Sarah. *Interior Design with Feng Shui*, Rider, London, 1987

Rybczynski, Witold. *Home,* Penguin, New York, 1986

St. Aubyn, Lorna. *Rituals for Everyday Living*, Piatkus, London, 1994

St. James, Elaine. *Living the Simple Life*, Hyperion, New York, 1996

St. James, Elaine. *Simplify Your Life*, Hyperion, New York, 1994

Sardello, Robert. *Facing the World with Soul*, Lindisfarne Press, New York, 1992

Schiff, Francine. *Food for Solitude, Element*, Shaftesbury, 1992

Shurety, Sarah. *Feng Shui for Your Home*, Rider, London, 1997

Smith, Cyril W. & Best, Simon. *Electromagnetic Man*, Dent, London, 1989

Spear, William. *Feng Shui Made Easy*, Thorsons, London, 1995

Too, Lillian. *The Complete Illustrated Guide to Feng Shui*, Element, Shaftesbury, 1996

Uyldert, Mellie. *The Magic of Precious Stones*, Aquarian Press, Wellingborough, 1981

Verner Bonds, Lilian. *Discover the Magic of Colour*, Optima, London, 1993

Wildwood, Chrissie. Bloomsbury *Encyclopedia of Aromatherapy*, Bloomsbury, London, 1996

Wildwood, Chrissie. *Create Your Own Perfumes Using Essential Oils*, Piatkus, London, 1994

Worwood, Valerie Ann. *The Fragrant Mind*, Doubleday, London, 1995

Worwood, Valerie Ann. *The Fragrant Pharmacy*, Bantam, London, 1990

Worwood, Valerie Ann. *Fragrant Sensuality*, Bantam, London, 1993

index